The Life and Crimes of Railroad Bill

UNIVERSITY PRESS OF FLORIDA

Florida A&M University, Tallahassee
Florida Atlantic University, Boca Raton
Florida Gulf Coast University, Ft. Myers
Florida International University, Miami
Florida State University, Tallahassee
New College of Florida, Sarasota
University of Central Florida, Orlando
University of Florida, Gainesville
University of North Florida, Jacksonville
University of South Florida, Tampa
University of West Florida, Pensacola

Life and Crimes
of Railroad Bill

Legendary African American Desperado

Larry L. Massey

University Press of Florida
Gainesville · Tallahassee · Tampa · Boca Raton
Pensacola · Orlando · Miami · Jacksonville · Ft. Myers · Sarasota

Library of Congress Control Number: 2015936114
ISBN 978-0-8130-6120-7

The University Press of Florida is the scholarly publishing agency for the State
University System of Florida, comprising Florida A&M University, Florida
Atlantic University, Florida Gulf Coast University, Florida International
University, Florida State University, New College of Florida, University of
Central Florida, University of Florida, University of North Florida, University
of South Florida, and University of West Florida.

University Press of Florida
15 Northwest 15th Street
Gainesville, FL 32611-2079
http://www.upf.com

In loving memory of Bertha Howell Massey
and Barbara Massey Eubanks

Contents

Preface and Acknowledgments

Railroad Bill—an African American outlaw who terrorized parts of Alabama and Florida in the late nineteenth century— did not kill Benjamin Dickson, as my mother believed for most of her life. A man named Thomas Johnson killed her maternal great-grandfather.

My mother's misunderstanding began in the late 1920s, when she was about ten years of age. At that time the legend of Railroad Bill was capturing the imagination of the Deep South, conveyed in the lyrics of a folk ballad with a bad-man theme. My mother enjoyed singing it with playmates and some of her eleven siblings. She also enjoyed listening when her father picked a banjo with friends who occasionally gathered with musical instruments on the veranda of their Mississippi farmhouse. One of their favorite songs was "Railroad Bill."

On one occasion when my mother was on a visit to her maternal grandmother's home, she was taken aside and shown the shirt that Dickson had worn on the day he died. With amazement the girl viewed the bullet holes through which death had entered three decades before. She also listened attentively when her grandmother told stories of two killings at Bluff Springs, Florida. They involved Railroad Bill and Ben Dickson, and they occurred within a few days of each other. In the first, Railroad Bill shot Sheriff Edward McMillan one night near the railroad station. Dickson, Johnson, and another friend retrieved the wounded officer, who died a few hours later. But only four days later in a confrontation at the railroad station, Johnson shot and killed Dickson. My mother's young mind somehow merged the stories, concluding that the outlaw made popular in song had killed her great-grandfather. Her mistake continued throughout most of her life, primarily because her father never allowed the family to discuss their paternal heritage.

An article in *The Buffalo (N.Y.) Express* on July 16, 1895, provides additional information on Dickson and Railroad Bill. It states that Dickson, who was in business with a man named Hughes, brought Railroad Bill from North Carolina to Alabama to work in a Baldwin County turpentine operation (evidently Hughes and Dickson jointly transferred their turpentine labor crew from the Carolinas). Dickson is quoted as saying that Railroad Bill "was one of the most inoffensive negroes he ever knew until recently." But that inoffensiveness ended after Railroad Bill was thrown from a moving train by L&N brakemen, leading to a personal vendetta against the company. Johnson was a detective seeking a large reward offered for Railroad Bill's capture. He became embroiled in an argument with Dickson that led to blows. Dickson attacked Johnson with a knife; Johnson killed Dickson with a revolver.

I also grew up believing Railroad Bill was the killer of Dickson. But when one of my older cousins commented that it was her understanding that "Dickson had raised Railroad Bill," I began a search of the historical record. I not only discovered the fate of Dickson; I also discovered an intriguing story about the notorious man known as Railroad Bill.

This book presents the results of that research. It is based on 1890s newspaper articles published during or just after Railroad Bill's criminal career and on some early-twentieth-century information published by people involved in the outlaw's story. Unfortunately, newspaper articles were inconsistent and often contradictory in presenting details for each major event. They nevertheless formed a mosaic from which details in the following chapters were chosen.

Many individuals assisted in my work. With enduring gratitude I sincerely thank Angela Balter, Tracey Berezansky, Katherine Blood, Jeanette Bornholt, John Burrison, Neal Collier, Lisa Dixon, Linda Douglass, Nancy Dupree, Carol Ellis, Laura Farah, Samantha Feisel, Todd Harvey, Wanda Hadley, Sian Hunter, Stephanye Hunter, Katherine Johnson, Nona Johnson, Jonathan Lawrence, Meredith McLemore, Bertha Massey, Margaret Massey, Michael Massey, Cathy McKinley, Dan McMillan, Thomas E. McMillan Jr., Mike Odom, Wesley Odom, Herbert Prytherch, Jerry Simmons, Allison Sinrod, Evan Strohl, Linda Tyler, Marthe Walters, Voncille Ward, Jacquelyn Wilson, and Alexa Zelinski.

I would also like to thank the following institutions and their employees for assistance with research: Alabama Department of Archives and History, Baldwin County Department of Archives and History, D. W. McMillan Trust, Escambia County

Historical Society, Friends of the St. John's Cemetery Foundation, Jacksonville Public Library, Library of Congress, Miami-Dade Public Library, Mobile Public Library, New Orleans Public Library, Old Dominion University Library, Pensacola Historical Society, the *Fairhope Courier*, Thomas E. McMillan Museum, and West Florida Genealogy Library.

Introduction

Alabama's Bad Man

Paul McCartney could not have known his adventure would give rise to the world's most popular rock band. But after cycling from Liverpool to Woolton, England, on July 6, 1957, he attended a fair being held on the grounds of St. Peter's Church and was introduced to another young and ambitious musician named John Lennon. That meeting heralded the birth of the legendary Beatles.[1]

But another legend was also heralded at Woolton that Saturday. He was portrayed in the lyrics of a folk ballad that Lennon sang with his newly formed band, the Quarrymen, while McCartney was in the audience. But the ballad, or "skiffle" as that genre of music is known in Great Britain, was not English in origin. Nor was it European. It was born before the turn of the century on the lips of African Americans living in the pine forests of Alabama and Florida. The singer who would soon become an entertainment icon was celebrating an infamous African American train robber known in Dixie as Railroad Bill.[2]

The outlaw's infamous journey began when Captain Theodore J. Hughes, a Confederate veteran and entrepreneur, conveyed him from South Carolina to the piney woods of Baldwin County, Alabama, to work at his turpentine camp. "Railroad's skill as a workman is on record," the Montgomery *Daily Advertiser* wrote on April 10, 1895, "and it's way up at the top notch." In 1894 the turpentine laborer was still working for Hughes, but at a camp at Bluff Springs, Florida.[3]

The Hughes Turpentine Company was situated near the limits of Bluff Springs and plagued by difficulties having nothing to do with harvesting and distilling pine pitch for turpentine and tar. Strife had developed between predominantly black laborers living in the company quarters of Hughes and the predominantly white townspeople living in Bluff Springs. In 1892 unknown parties fired into the camp and wounded three men. In 1893 a Hughes employee murdered the town marshal. Three nights later, an African American church burned and an African American bystander was killed in his doorway. In 1894 an Escambia County deputy sheriff attempted to arrest the individual who would become Railroad Bill for carrying a repeating rifle without a permit. An exchange of gunshots erupted, making the turpentine worker a wanted man in Florida. He left Bluff Springs and became "one of the most desperate characters ever known in this section."[4]

After leaving Bluff Springs, Railroad Bill organized a band of thieves and robbed freight being shipped on boxcars of the Louisville and Nashville Railroad (L&N) in southern Alabama between Mobile and Flomaton. They stole merchandise valued at thousands of dollars, causing the L&N to dispatch detectives

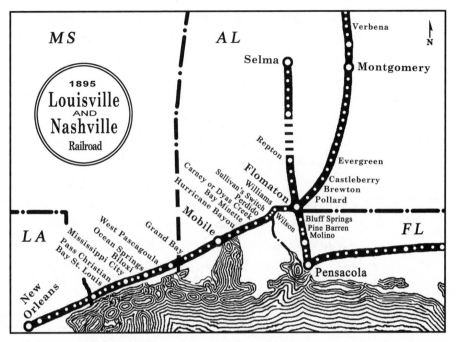

Louisville and Nashville Railroad stations associated with the story of
Railroad Bill.

to investigate. Rewards were also publicly offered for Railroad
Bill's apprehension that increased in value as his crimes pro-
gressed from stealing to wounding trainmen to murder. Eventually the amount of reward money attracted lawmen, bounty
hunters, and Pinkerton agents from as far away as Chicago.[5]

Railroad Bill proved exceedingly difficult to capture. The
L&N hired informants to gain information on his whereabouts
and plans. The most noted undercover agent was Mark Stinson, who successfully gained the outlaw's trust and provided
information to the company. But then he mysteriously disappeared, leading the press to assume that Railroad Bill had

learned of his double-dealing, killed him, and hidden his body. The historical record, however, points a guilty finger at railroad detectives.[6]

Railroad Bill's most celebrated escape was a five-day chase on foot in the swamps of Escambia and Conecuh Counties, Alabama, in which he was pursued by scores of armed men with bloodhounds. His inexplicable exploits led to the emergence of numerous folk stories purporting him to have a supernatural power to confound pursuers by disappearing or transforming into an animal or an inanimate object. A folk ballad with a badman theme also emerged and would remain popular decades after the outlaw's death. Folklorists studied the ballad in the 1910s; lyrics were collected in the 1920s that are archived in the Library of Congress; artists recorded it in the 1920s and 1930s for commercial distribution; U.S. troops introduced it to Europe in the 1940s; and a skiffle movement gained popularity in the 1950s in England, promoted in part by a rendition of "Railroad Bill" by Lonnie Donegan, the "King of Skiffle." Music in that decade also nourished young English performers who would make a professional mark in the 1960s. The most notable were Paul McCartney and John Lennon with their legendary band, the Beatles.[7]

Although the lyrics and tune of "Railroad Bill" have delighted audiences on both sides of the Atlantic, a book-length history of the actual person and his criminal career has not been forthcoming. Several explanations seem to apply. An important one may have been an act passed by the Alabama General Assembly during Railroad Bill's criminal career. It prohibited the "printing, publishing, selling, offering to sell or otherwise disposing of books, pamphlets or tracts containing the history of any man popularly known as an outlaw." To remedy the obvious oversight, this book presents a comprehensive history based primarily on articles published in the 1890s or early twentieth century. It is a factual history of the individual, the legend, and the song known as "Railroad Bill."[8]

Becoming
Railroad Bill

1

~

An Eyewitness Interview

Little is known about the individual before he became infamous by the nickname Railroad Bill. Newspaper articles described him as bold, powerful, and athletic. He followed a circus early in life and may have worked as a railroad hand before becoming a turpentine laborer. He could read and write. He demonstrated a talent for showmanship. He used numerous nicknames. His real name, however, is unknown. He apparently had no immediate family in the turpentine camps in which he lived and worked, and no family member stepped forward after his death to claim his body. But authorities in Selma, Alabama, declared that he had once lived there and still had family living there. Historian James Penick describes Railroad Bill as an outlaw who appeared before the public "with no past and no future, and no other name."[1]

Rev. Robert W. Brooks was the postmaster at Bluff Springs in the 1890s and knew the turpentine worker who would become Railroad Bill. He said the outlaw-to-be "would often draw the figure of a bird as a part of the address" on letters he mailed. He "seemed to be peacefully disposed." He could perform sleight-of-hand tricks, which "the white children were said to have been fond of."[2]

Clara Phillips Wolfe met Alabama's Bad Man in 1895 when she was five years of age. In 1977 she spoke with a reporter about that encounter.[3]

"Railroad Bill was a black man," Clara said, "a black man who turned out to be an oddball."[4]

Clara lived at Perdido, a community in Alabama about two miles west of the Florida state line, thirty-eight miles northeast of Mobile. The farmhouse in which she lived was the same one visited by Railroad Bill in 1895. It overlooked a wooded lane leading northward about two hundred yards, almost to a railroad track, part of L&N's Mobile and Montgomery Division in the 1890s. Freight shipped in boxcars along that line became the object of Railroad Bill's criminal ambition.

Railroad Bill came to Clara's house on Saturday, March 9, 1895. It was only three days after he fought a gunfight with trainmen at a small railway station twenty miles southwest of Perdido, known in the 1890s as Hurricane Bayou. He typically carried two large-caliber pistols, an equally large-caliber Winchester rifle, and a cartridge belt of .44-caliber ammunition. Those prompted the Montgomery *Daily Advertiser* to dub him "a walking arsenal." But on this occasion he was without his coveted rifle, having lost it in the gunfight. Clara's family owned a potential replacement.[5]

Jiles Lofton Phillips, Clara's eldest brother, had taken the rifle into the woods for target practice that Saturday. Railroad Bill may have seen him using it, since he confronted the teenager at the end of the lane nearest the railroad track. The outlaw then grabbed for the rifle, but Jiles dodged the assault and hurried home.[6]

In ten to fifteen minutes, Railroad Bill came to the Phillips home and met Clara's father, James Phillips. Clara said the fugitive had "his hat all tied up and his face all tied up with a red handkerchief." She didn't explain, but the handkerchief was not to disguise his identity, or he would also have brandished a weapon. Instead, it must have served as a bandage for a facial wound. Accounts stated that he had been "badly wounded" in the face during the gunfight at Hurricane Bayou. And a month later, an L&N circular described him as having "a fresh scar on left cheek, extending from front of face and leaving off under left ear."[7]

When Railroad Bill asked for food, James retrieved a plate from his wife, Susan, in the kitchen, and gave it to their unusual visitor, who was probably on or near the breezeway—a passage through the house used by the family as a porch. It was common in that era for travelers to stop at farmhouses and ask, or offer to pay, for food. Yet it seems odd that Railroad Bill would approach inoffensively after attempting to steal the rifle from Jiles. It also seems strange that James would show hospitality. Clara didn't comment on that aspect of her narrative, but she did state that she remembered little from that day, and most of what she knew was told to her by her family later in life.[8]

Clara's father probably knew or suspected who the individual was and the danger he posed. The L&N had been seeking the outlaw's capture for several months and had issued a notice warning employees of his danger. Also, accounts of the gunfight at Hurricane Bayou had appeared in newspapers, which had undoubtedly stirred conversation within the Perdido community.[9]

Interestingly, Clara's account no longer mentions her father after he gave food to the outlaw. Perhaps James stepped away to attend to a chore or to alert the authorities. For whatever reason, Clara's focus turned to her mother. After Railroad Bill ate part of his food, he complained about its quality and asked for raw eggs to take with him to boil. Mrs. Phillips retrieved six farm eggs that Railroad Bill received in one large hand.[10]

"Where's your boy?" the outlaw demanded. "That's who I want to see!"[11]

"Nobody's gonna get any gun," Susan retorted.[12]

Anticipating a confrontation, Mrs. Phillips went into the house and warned Jiles. Rifle in hand, he fled through a rear exit and hurried southward about a mile to reach Perdido Missionary Baptist Church. The congregation was holding a Saturday Bible study, but after hearing his story a group of armed men made their way back to the Phillips farm.[13]

Meanwhile, Susan, with Clara at her side, returned to their strange visitor. But when he pulled a large revolver and waved it at them, it terrified the child, who remembered running hand-in-hand with her mother. That left Sam, Clara's brother of about fourteen years of age, and a family friend, a boy of about the same age, with Railroad Bill. He forced them into a room-by-room search for the rifle.[14]

"Tell them to get that gun!" he shouted. "I want that rifle! I got to have that rifle! You do know where that rifle is!!"[15]

The desperado also fired over the boys' heads, splintering a picket in the family's fence. That shot, and perhaps others, may have been to scare the children or to threaten Clara's father, assuming he was planning to return in defense of his family. But in the end, Railroad Bill left without the rifle, without physically harming anyone, and before the men from the church arrived.[16]

"I think all that was awful," Clara said. "I don't know whether Railroad Bill was crazy or mean."[17]

But the outlaw's pursuit of a rifle that day didn't end at the Phillips farm. Around sundown Railroad Bill and an accomplice went to the farm of a Mr. Williamson, also near Perdido, knowing the farmer owned a "fine Winchester." In finding him at work in his barn, Railroad Bill took a stand at the front door of the house while the accomplice entered and stole the rifle amid screams from Williamson's wife and daughters. The farmer heard their cries and ran to their assistance. But as he turned a corner of the house, the accomplice was exiting with the rifle, and both assailants fired on him, forcing him back into the barn. The Montgomery *Daily Advertiser* commented that "it is probable that they did not intend to kill [Williamson] since both missed him."[18]

The Winchester rifle, instead of murder, was clearly Railroad Bill's objective at both houses. A rifle was more accurate than a revolver at medium to long range, and a repeating rifle could fire more than twice as many rounds as a revolver before reloading. If the desperado had been approached by a well-armed posse, the rifle could have made the difference between freedom and capture, life and death.

2

Circus Performer

Circuses and road shows were common attractions in the second half of the nineteenth century. Traveling by steamboat, train, and wagon, they visited towns and cities across the landscape, providing entertainment on demand. They also presented an exotic lifestyle that captured the imagination of young men with a hunger for adventure. One of those was Railroad Bill. While following a circus, he apparently developed an athletic prowess and a talent for showmanship. He could "perform many feats of contortion and juggling with two pistols buckled about his waist and a Winchester slung over his shoulders." He was able to "stand flat-footed and turn air springs, either forward or backward." He could "pick up a keg of nails in his teeth and throw it over his head. . . . In lifting and throwing heavy weights his feats are of the same surprising order."[1]

Samuel H. Chambers, telegraph operator in Mobile, provided this anecdote of Railroad Bill's showmanship, which occurred shortly before the showman became an outlaw:

One day Railroad appeared at the depot dressed rather more tidily than the average negro, wearing a silk, stovepipe hat, a little the worse for wear, and a Prince Albert coat. He seemed to be in rather straitened circumstances, though, and remarked to the crowd which surrounded him that if a small collection would be secured for his benefit, he would show them some new tricks. Accordingly several gentlemen "chipped" in and about 40 or 50 cents was secured for the negro, whereupon he proceeded to do as he had promised. The first thing he did was to secure a large saucer and shove it into his mouth, which seemed to require very little effort upon his part. He performed several other feats at the depot and wound up his exhibition by going across the street to the office of the New Orleans brewery, where he picked up a large bucket, almost full of water and drank the entire contents; then, passing his hand to and fro over his stomach several times, so as to give the water a sort of "presto change" kind of movement, he discharged the entire contents of the bucket from his mouth.

Mobile *Daily Register*, March 10, 1896

The circus would not bring Railroad Bill to live and work in southern Alabama. That honor fell to Captain Theodore J. Hughes, a turpentine entrepreneur born in North Carolina and educated at Chapel Hill. During the Civil War, Hughes had served "two years in England as the agent of his state, and was latter appointed commander of the blockade runner Advance, plying between Wilmington and Liverpool." After the war he operated a turpentine business in Baldwin County and brought several laborers from South Carolina to work in his camp. One of them was Railroad Bill.[2]

Hughes left the turpentine business around 1882 and moved to Mobile to work as a cotton broker. Around 1891 he returned to his former line of work, this time at Bluff Springs, Florida. The camp had been founded by James H. Grimlar on land purchased from C. A. Moreno in 1890. It was known as the Hughes and Grimlar Turpentine Company in 1892, and the Hughes Turpentine Company in 1895. Hughes operated the camp until his death in 1896.[3]

An L&N detective from Montgomery named Thomas J. Watts was tasked with apprehending Railroad Bill. He described the outlaw as follows:

> Five feet 7 inches in height, aged about twenty eight years, color nearly dark, build chunky. The most peculiar feature of him is his neck. It is said he can throw his head back and pull his collar over his head. He is quick as a flash and active as a kitten. He will not let any stranger get close to him.
>
> New Orleans *Times-Democrat*, April 11, 1895

The unusual flexibility in Railroad Bill's neck indicates that he was double-jointed: having the genetic ability (hypermobility) to flex a joint beyond its normal range. That was corroborated by a report that he could "perform many feats of contortion" and could "lift one leg over his head and standing by a wall, the inner sides of both legs will be pressed against it."[4]

A telegraph operator in Montgomery named Mr. Seale described the outlaw this way:

> Five feet six inches tall, weighs about 140 or 145 pounds; face dark yellow, as if sunburned or smoked; breast and stomach to the waist light yellow; uncommonly high cheek bones and broad face; small mouth with rather thick lips. When at Bay Minette last had a fresh-looking scar on the left cheek, evidently extending from the front of the face and leaving off just under the left ear. He wore a hickory shirt, open from throat to waist; small narrow brimmed slouch hat; small, dark sack coat, which looked like a summer coat, but thicker; had on no undershirt; pantaloons looked like grey jeans; wore No. 7 brogan shoes, cut in slits extending from the toe lip to the instep. Both feet make a good impression in the ground.
>
> Mobile *Daily Register*, April 12, 1895

Railroad Bill's light complexion suggested that he was mulatto. James I. McKinney, superintendent of the L&N's Mobile and Montgomery Division, also mentioned Bill's light complexion in his description:

> [He is] 26 or 27 years of age, 5 feet 6 inches tall, weighs between 150 and 160 pounds, complexion dark yellow, high cheek bones, broad face, thick lips, and has a daring expression. Has a fresh scar on left cheek, extending from front of face and leaving off under left ear.
>
> Greenville *Advocate*, April 17, 1895

These three descriptions define an individual five feet, six or seven inches in height and weighing 140 to 160 pounds.

Railroad Bill, however, was larger. The undertaker measured his corpse as five feet, eleven inches tall and weighing 165 pounds.[5]

The nickname "Railroad Bill" evolved after the turpentine worker left Bluff Springs and became an outlaw. According to the L&N, other nicknames the turpentine laborer was known to use were Zeb, C. S. Slater, and Colonel Slater. C. S. Slater may have stood for Colonel S. Slater. "Colonel" was a moniker loosely used in the Deep South to convey respect for a man's ability. Rube Burrow, Alabama's most notorious railroad bandit, was sometimes called Colonel Rube, though he never served as a military officer.[6]

At the beginning of Railroad Bill's criminal career, reporters didn't know the outlaw's name or nickname. Consequently, in reporting his crimes, they attributed them generically to the work of a tramp. But after the gunfight at Hurricane Bayou, a fight that made him "an object of interest to the press of three states," reporters began to call him "Railroad." A month later, after he killed a man near Bay Minette, Alabama, the press described him as a "desperado known only by the name of 'Railroad Bill.'"[7]

W. B. Dinwiddie lived in southern Alabama as a boy and remembered Railroad Bill in the turpentine business being called "Railroad Time." But Dinwiddie said two railroad detectives investigating the individual somehow substituted "Bill" for "Time," with the former becoming more popular.[8]

The detectives Dinwiddie referred to may have been two Mobile police officers named Edward Morris and James Donoghue. They were assigned in August 1894 as special detectives to investigate an incident on the L&N in which a Winchester-wielding individual commandeered a train and forced the crew to pull out of the Hurricane Bayou station, eighteen miles northeast of Mobile. This occurred at the same time that W. B. Jones, president of the African American Longshoremen's Union, was causing trouble for the L&N and the city police in Mobile. Jones happened to be nicknamed Railroad Bill. His offense was to post a circular offering free lunch and beer at the union hall for longshoremen desiring better wages for loading bananas from vessels at the docks into railway cars to be conveyed to northern states to be sold. The L&N would deem possible union wage demands and work stoppages as trouble, especially with a product as perishable as bananas. City police also viewed the circular as trouble since it coincided with a violent labor dispute that was occurring in New Orleans at that time. That dispute had become so severe that the governor of Louisiana had threatened to activate the state militia to prevent a race war. Morris and Donoghue may have simply dubbed the "Railroad Time" troublemaker at Hurricane Bayou after the "Railroad Bill" troublemaker in Mobile.[9]

The outlaw's real name is also unclear, since at least five real names were proposed by the press. The first was "Morris Salter" (also stated as Salters). It appeared in the Montgomery *Daily Advertiser* on March 12, 1895, five days after the gunfight at Hurricane Bayou. But on April 9, 1895, two days after the murder of a deputy near Bay Minette, the Mobile *Daily Register* and the Pensacola *Daily News* used the surname "Slater" for Railroad Bill. The following day the *Daily Advertiser* followed suit by using the same surname. In addition, the Mobile and Montgomery Division of the L&N also used "Morris Slater" in a wanted poster. The division's office at Union Station in Montgomery had received instructions from headquarters in Louisville on April 9 to offer a reward of $350 for the desperado, dead or alive. The money would be paid in addition to a $150 reward being offered by the State of Alabama. "Morris Slater" had become the standard for the outlaw. But it was not the last real name proposed by seemingly reliable sources.[10]

A third name for Railroad Bill was published at Brewton, Alabama, just after the outlaw's death:

> Learning that Mr. S. B. Botts could give a bit of Railroad's history, a News man interviewed him yesterday. He tells us his real name is Bill McCoy and that he brought him to this county from Coldwater, Fla., about eighteen years ago. That Bill was in his employ two years. He was a young negro then, about eighteen years old.
>
> Brewton *Pine Belt News*, March 10, 1896

Botts estimated the outlaw's age at death to be about thirty-six, which contrasts with the L&N's estimate of about twenty-nine years. Also notable is that Botts waited until the excitement following Railroad Bill's demise to reveal his information.[11]

A fourth proposed name for Railroad Bill appeared in a news brief from Montgomery announcing his death: "William Brown, a colored man, known as 'Railroad Bill,' the terror of train crews for miles around." No information on the derivation of the name was provided.[12]

Will Barker was a fifth name proposed for the outlaw. It appeared in several news releases from Selma about seven months before Railroad Bill's death. Authorities in the city were convinced that Railroad Bill was Barker, a former resident who still had a wife and sister living there. Barker had worked for a railroad before being dismissed after meat went missing from a railway car. That incident may have been indirectly mentioned in an article originating in Mobile, which stated that Railroad Bill came "to the section in which he was killed some years ago from Birmingham, where he had a difficulty with a policeman."[13]

Railroad Bill might have been Morris Salter, Morris Slater, Bill McCoy, William Brown, Will Barker, or some other individual. He might have come from Florida, Alabama, South Carolina, or some other location. He might have been fired by a railroad company. He might have had a problem with a policeman in Birmingham. He might have had a wife and sister living at Selma. About the only thing that can be stated with certainty is that whoever he was and wherever he was from, apprehending him would prove more difficult than anyone could have imagined at the time of the gunfight at Hurricane Bayou.

3

Trouble on the Railroad

Railroads across the United States were under siege in the 1890s. Armed robbery of express and mail cars, depredation of freight cars, theft by employees and passengers, and train wrecking for robbery by depraved individuals forced railroad officials to police their lines. The companies contracted with special detectives and hired full-time detectives to cross state lines and work with local authorities to capture and prosecute offenders. The officials remained skeptical, however, that local authorities and courts would aggressively prosecute local suspects charged with railroad crime. An official with a railroad said:

> It is a fact juries very seldom find defendants guilty when arrested at the instance of a railroad company. This is probably due to the widely existing prejudice against railroad corporations. Our evidence against a trespasser must be of the strongest character in order to win the

case; stronger, in fact, than would be necessary to convict
a prisoner arrested under other circumstances.

Atlanta Constitution, March 28, 1894

The public generally viewed railroads with disdain. They believed the companies were controlled by robber barons who
had influenced legislation to take private property for rights-
of-way and then operated their lines as monopolies, charging
exorbitant fees for transportation. That attitude may explain
some of the public's fascination with railroad bandits such as
Jesse James and Rube Burrow, who were sometimes viewed as
Robin Hood types. But Railroad Bill did not achieve that sta-
tus within the Anglo-American segment of the population. Besides residing on the opposite side of a large racial divide, any
empathy he may have engendered was quickly extinguished
when he killed a well-liked member of a posse near Bay Minette. Burrow experienced something similar in 1889 when he
killed a popular postmaster in northern Alabama.[1]

Railroad Bill traveled like a tramp, yet he was not a tramp by
the general definition: someone searching for work or enjoying
the transient lifestyle. Moreover, he was more heavily armed
than the average tramp and could be more belligerent. Early in
April 1895, a brakeman found him on a train traveling between
Flomaton and Bluff Springs, "sitting between two cars with his
Winchester on his knees." The brakeman raised his lantern and
commanded him to get up. "This is Railroad," the outlaw replied, "and I don't want any trouble with you. Tell the conductor not to come around me." There was no more trouble.[2]

Tramping had evolved after the Civil War as people began to
roam from town to town inside empty boxcars. It was a dangerous means of travel, yet it was expedient for those who could

not afford otherwise. The Panic of 1893, a severe depression in the nation's economy that led to high rates of unemployment, further encouraged hordes of men and some women to flood the railways as tramps searching for work. A newspaper commented in 1894 that "it is safe to say that there is not a freight train running that has not ten or a dozen people on, stealing rides." In 1899 a magazine added that riding inside an empty boxcar at night "is comparatively easy to do; on many roads it is possible to travel this way, undisturbed, till morning." Railroad Bill's lifestyle mimicked that of a tramp, which made him difficult to apprehend. Allan Pinkerton of the Pinkerton National Detective Agency noted that with time he could probably catch almost any type of criminal except a tramp: "One day he is in a barn, the next in a haystack, and the next Heaven only knows where he is, for he has probably got on to the railroad, and there you might as well look for a lost pin."[3]

Crimes Railroad Bill committed on the L&N between 1894 and 1896 encouraged the State of Alabama in 1898 to pass a law that prohibited tramping on railways within the state. Three years later, Superintendent McKinney commented on crime during Railroad Bill's era and the subsequent merits of the new law:

Previous to December, 1898, our road between Mobile and Montgomery was infested with tramps. Many times they were so numerous that the train crews could not control them. Depredations were committed by them in every imaginable form—breaking into cars, stealing freight, wrecking trains, etc. On one occasion, between Flomaton and Mobile, they took possession of one of our trains, shooting the brakeman and throwing him off; and at another time shooting in the knee a brakeman who had put some of them off; again, four of them shot one of our freight conductors. When they were put off trains they would frequently place obstructions on the track, causing wrecks; hence the necessity of the above law. . . . Since the law went into effect we have arrested and convicted 300 offenders, and the good results of this action have been far-reaching. We have noticed a wonderful decrease in the number of cars broken into and robbed. We have not had an attempt at a train wreck since the law was passed.

The Railway Conductor, 1901

Railroad Bill's gang operated much like other freight-car gangs in many parts of the nation. A prominent gang until their arrest in 1897 was led by Walter Bohannon near Dalton, Georgia. After finding someone willing to buy stolen merchandise, the gang sent a couple of men to reconnoiter around a train stopped at night at a coal shoot at Varnell, Georgia, eight miles north of Dalton. A car was selected on the basis of emanating odors such as tobacco or coffee, the door to that car was breached, and the men entered and waited until the train was under way. Then they lit a candle and selected cases of merchandise to stack in front of the door. Twenty minutes after leaving Varnell—the time it took for the train to pass a location where other gang members were hidden in the woods with a wagon—they pushed the crates out of the door. The men with the wagon gathered the merchandise, placed it in bags, and transported it to a home or hid it in the woods until it was sold. The shipping crates were burned near the track to destroy identifying information. As the train slowed to enter Dalton, the men inside the car would jump out and, if time and conditions permitted, reattach the seal on the door to delay discovery of their theft. Bohannon handled all sales, and each man was paid a percentage of the profit depending on his participation in the crime.[4]

Although twentieth-century folklore sometimes portrayed Railroad Bill as a type of Robin Hood who stole from a rich railroad to give to the poor, it would have been difficult to persuade men to undertake the arduous task of robbing trains for charity, especially when the penalty was incarceration at hard labor.[5]

Railroad Bill probably sold most of his stolen merchandise to proprietors of company stores in the turpentine and timber camps that dotted the piney backwoods. A typical camp included cabins in which employees lived and a company store in which they purchased goods, often on credit. Edward Leigh McMillan, a Brewton attorney whose father was killed by Railroad Bill, stated that "it was believed by many that he had the assistance of certain white people to whom he was giving or selling very cheap, the goods and merchandise that were stolen from the railroad." The white people to whom McMillan referred may have been associated with company stores. An L&N conductor seems to have corroborated McMillan's statement. The trainman stated that Railroad Bill had "a habit of getting on the passenger trains at Hurricane Bayou and Dolive and leaving at Williams Station, Carneys Station or Perdido." He added that "after leaving the train [Railroad Bill] generally goes through the country, frequenting the turpentine camps as far south as Bluff Springs."[6]

4

The Desperado Wyatt Tate

Railroad Bill wasn't the only African American outlaw to raise the ire of lawmen in southern Alabama in the 1890s. Wyatt Tate (sometimes spelled Tait) foreshadowed the notorious desperado, becoming infamous in Monroe County a year before Railroad Bill became infamous in Baldwin County, some sixty miles to the south. Tate and Railroad Bill produced eerily similar résumés. Each violently resisted arrest; each armed himself with a rifle, several pistols, and copious ammunition; each killed a deputy sheriff and ambushed and killed a high sheriff; each successfully evaded multiple posses; each incurred bounties offered for his head dead or alive; and each suffered a violent death. Tate, however, wasn't known for robbing trains, nor did he become a folk legend.

Tate's career began on March 24, 1894, when Constable William Ikner attempted to serve an arrest warrant on him for stealing a horse from another African American. Ikner deputized his brother and two neighbors. Law officers were scarce in rural areas, so it was customary to deputize citizens to temporarily serve on dangerous missions. A posse was justified in Tate's case. Not only was he dangerous, but nine days earlier another Monroe County constable had run into trouble while attempting to serve a warrant alone:

> While attempting to serve a warrant on a negro near town, charged with larceny, Friday evening, several negroes interfered, overpowering Constable Watson and severely bruised him about the head and face. Apprehending not [sic] trouble, he went entirely unarmed and was consequently unable to defend himself. He returned with reinforcements and captured all the parties implicated, against whom several additional charges were lodged.
>
> Monroe *Journal*, March 15, 1894

When Ikner's posse arrived at Tate's residence in Flat Creek Swamp near Finchburg, the suspect refused arrest and fired on the men through a small hole in his cabin. The posse scurried behind an outbuilding in front of the cabin, and there Ikner made two serious mistakes. First, he allowed both of his neighbors to go for reinforcements, whereas one should have stayed to help watch the cabin. Second, he and his brother remained behind the outbuilding, whereas they should have separated to cover the front and back of the cabin in case Tate attempted to escape. Consequently, from their position they did not see the suspect leave through a secret exit at the back of the house. They also did not see him circle behind them. From a distance of fifty yards, Tate shot Ikner in the back of the head, killing the constable who would be eulogized as "a good and peaceable citizen."[1]

The next day at Monroeville, the seat of Monroe County, Sheriff J. D. Foster organized a posse that searched for Tate but without success. Citizens raised three hundred dollars for the fugitive's capture, dead or alive. They also sent a telegram to Governor Thomas G. Jones, asking that the state offer a similar amount. Rewards offered publicly for a suspect dead or alive were the equivalent of the individual having been tried in absentia, found guilty, and sentenced to death. Tate had become legal game for anyone willing to take up arms.[2]

Ten days after Ikner's death, Foster organized another posse for a night raid. According to the following day's paper, Tate "has sworn not to be taken alive, and has fortified his place, situated in Flat creek swamp, and, armed with a forty-four-caliber rifle, pistols, and four hundred rounds of ammunition, defies arrest." Presumably, a night raid increased the likelihood of finding a fugitive at a predictable location and off guard, perhaps asleep. It also seemingly reduced the likelihood that the posse would be discovered and the fugitive forewarned.[3]

Foster's posse arrived at Tate's residence around 10:00 p.m. and found it unoccupied. But while the men lingered outside the cabin in the darkness, a shot rang out. It was fired by someone in nearby bushes, and everyone believed it was Tate. The shooter, nevertheless, escaped.[4]

The bullet struck Foster in the arm above the elbow. The wound could have been successfully treated, but in the confusion the men thought that he had been wounded in the body, and appropriate medical attention wasn't given. The sheriff bled to death. The mortal mistake was not discovered until the next day when the body was being prepared for burial. Foster left a wife and two children.[5]

The murder of Ikner and Foster outraged the public. According to the Mobile *Daily Register*, "much indignation now exists in Monroe county by reason of the foul and wholly unprovoked murder, and if the negro is caught he may be lynched." The newspaper added two days later that "in all probability Tate would be burned at the stake, whether captured dead or alive. The feeling is so intense against the murderer that such a move on the part of the outraged community would meet with but little resistance."[6]

Governor Jones appointed I. B. Slaughter, brother-in-law of the deceased Foster, to fulfill the remaining term of office. The governor also authorized a state reward for Tate's apprehension, making a total reward of about six hundred dollars.[7] One of Slaughter's first tasks as sheriff was to publish a description of Tate:

> Color dark ginger cake; about 5 feet 8 inches in height; weight about 150 pounds; scar on top of head; one eyetooth out; one ankle scarred from old burn; has been shot with small shot, one shot lodging on side of neck just below ear; wears No. 9 shoe; scar on back of neck caused by burn; 32 years of age; prominent cheek bones and sharp chin; very thin mustache; eyes full. I will pay Five Hundred Dollars Reward for the capture of Wyatt Tate.
>
> Monroe *Journal*, April 26, 1894

Several citizen posses searched for the outlaw. One was composed of two African Americans, James Dunklin and Carey Willis. On the afternoon of May 4 they found Tate at home cooking a pig. They opened fire, causing the fugitive to run while firing left and right. Tate wounded Dunklin in the left arm and Willis in the back. A reinforced posse took up the chase, but Tate evaded capture.[8]

Murdock Fountain, a white farmer who also organized a citizen posse, had hunted Tate unsuccessfully for several weeks. Then his luck changed about a week after the Dunklin and Willis gunfight. He was attending a wake at the home of his brother-in-law Theo Marshall, near Repton, Alabama, when an African American man came around at 8:00 p.m. and told Fountain that he had met Tate, who was waiting in ambush. The farmer retrieved a double-barreled shotgun and began a search. In the shadows of shrubbery near an approach to the home, he found someone hiding. Twice he commanded the individual to show himself; twice there was no reply. Then he shouted, "Speak, or I will fire!" Instantly the men fired—Tate with a pistol, Fountain with a shotgun. Tate was struck and jumped for cover behind a small tree. Fountain fired his second barrel, striking Tate again, this time causing him to fall and exclaim, "Oh, Lord, you've killed me at last!" Although Tate continued to attempt to return fire, his pistol had been struck by Fountain's shot and rendered inoperable.[9]

Tate lived several more hours with wounds to the right arm and abdomen. During that time, according to the Monroe *Journal*, he "made a number of admissions, but exhibited the most unconquerable hatred toward the white people and all those who had aided in bringing him to his final account." Fountain transported the body to Monroeville the next day for official identification as generally required to receive a reward offered for a desperado.[10]

5

The Murder of Marshal Douglass

Railroad Bill was sometimes accused of a murder that he did not commit. This occurred as early as October 1894 when a train crew told a reporter that the outlaw "had committed a murder somewhere in Florida." But the historical record indicates that Railroad Bill did not kill anyone until April 1895. The error, nevertheless, was repeated by various authors during Railroad Bill's criminal career and afterward, leading some to inflate the number of men whom the desperado was thought to have killed. The misconception would even appear in the Railroad Bill's obituary published in the Atlanta *Constitution* on April 16, 1895: "Bill had killed the marshal of Bluff Springs, Fla."[1]

But Railroad Bill did not kill the town marshal of Bluff Springs. George Thomas, another turpentine worker, committed that murder. Thomas escaped after the killing and remained at large for years. During that time Railroad Bill, also a turpentine worker at Bluff Springs, became infamous and in

1895 killed a sheriff at Bluff Springs. The coincidence of both men having been turpentine workers in the same town and having killed law officers in the same town led some to believe that Thomas had killed the town marshal, had become infamous by the nickname Railroad Bill, and had killed the sheriff. But the murders were the work of two individuals.

The story of the marshal's murder began on May 22, 1893. Thomas entered town between 5:00 and 6:00 p.m. with a repeating rifle and fired four or five rounds at a target. Then he walked to the downtown store of the Hughes Turpentine Company, placed his rifle in the corner of a fence in front of the store, and stepped onto the gallery.[2]

Town Marshal David Douglass had been tending his garden when he heard Thomas's shots fired within the town limits, which violated a local ordinance. He proceeded with a citizen named Thomas Boutwell to the Hughes's store to investigate the turpentine worker. Neither Douglass nor Boutwell was armed, and when the marshal demanded that Thomas accompany them to the mayor's office, Thomas did not resist. But when they stepped into the street, Thomas stepped back, retrieved his rifle, and exclaimed that he had done nothing to deserve an arrest. He also threatened the marshal "not to come towards him." A moment later he fired, striking the officer in the breast, causing Douglass to fall in the street.[3]

Thomas turned his weapon on Boutwell, who was running up a side street. But the rifle malfunctioned, causing Thomas to pause and fix it before firing. The bullet ranged wide, and Boutwell escaped. Thomas then turned on others scurrying in the streets, including two shots at a Mr. Atkinson, who was coming out of his house fifty yards away.[4]

Thomas Douglass, Marshal Douglass's son, a "mere lad," was

clerking in the Hughes's store. When he heard shots and saw his father lying in the street, he retrieved a pistol in the store and fired five errant shots at Thomas, who was "standing over the prostrate body of Mr. Douglass," probably still firing at people on the street.[5]

Thomas then placed the muzzle to the head of the marshal lying in the street and pulled the trigger. But this time the rifle was out of ammunition and again did not fire. Thomas reloaded and began walking toward the nearby swamplands of the Escambia River. A posse gave chase, but it was late in the day and Thomas could not be found.[6]

A couple of days after Marshal Douglass was murdered, Sheriff John Collins of Santa Rosa County, Florida, sent a telegram to Sheriff Joseph Wilkins of Escambia County, Florida, stating that he had pursued Thomas into a swamp near Milton, Florida, and fired five shots at him. On May 24, two days after the marshal's murder, John Anderson was mistakenly arrested in New Orleans on suspicion of being George Thomas. Then on September 23, 1893, Joseph Mitchell was thought to be Thomas and arrested by the station agent at Deer Park on the Mobile and Ohio Railroad, about forty-three miles north of Mobile. Mitchell was transferred to jail in Mobile and interviewed by citizens from Bluff Springs. Although he resembled Thomas and stated that "if he had had his gun with him he would not have been taken, and intimated that he would have killed somebody," he was not Marshal Douglass's murderer. In February 1896 another person thought to be Thomas was arrested at Mississippi City on the Mississippi Gulf Coast. Mr. C. A. Moreno, a prominent merchant of Bluff Springs, traveled to see if he could identify the prisoner, but again it was not George Thomas. Finally, on July 30, 1897, four years after the murder, Sheriff D. Moore of Jackson County, Mississippi, arrested Thomas at Moss Point, forty miles west of Mobile. There was a five-hundred-dollar reward for the fugitive. Moore had been working in collaboration with Captain Peter Burke of the Burke Detective Agency in Mobile, who had been trailing Thomas for about three months. Thomas was expedited to Florida for prosecution.[7]

George Thomas had been working at Bluff Springs for less than a year before murdering Marshal Douglass. Although he was sometimes thought to be Railroad Bill, the two men differed in physical appearance. Thomas had "smooth features, long face," while Railroad Bill had "uncommonly high cheek bones and broad face; small mouth with rather thick lips." Thomas was "a little slow in movement and in speech," while Railroad Bill was "quick as a flash and active as a kitten." Thomas had "a large scar near the top of his forehead, made by a blow from an axe," whereas Railroad Bill had a "scar on the left cheek, evidently extending from the front of the face and leaving off just under the left ear."[8]

The misconception that Thomas was Railroad Bill would extend into the twentieth century, most notably by Carl Carmer in his 1934 classic, *Stars Fell on Alabama*. In presenting Railroad Bill's story, Carmer begins by describing an Escambia County turpentine worker named Morris Slater who came to town with a rifle and was confronted by a policeman. The officer demanded the rifle and grabbed for it. But the turpentine worker pulled away and fired, killing the policeman, before escaping to become infamous on the L&N as Railroad Bill. Carmer's narrative faithfully depicts the 1893 scene in Bluff Springs between George Thomas and Marshal Douglass, but George Thomas did not become Railroad Bill.[9]

II

Days of the Desperado

6

Gunfight at Hurricane Bayou

In his history of Escambia County, Alabama, Henderson A. Potter, a son of former slaves, comments on the most elusive of nineteenth-century African American desperados:

> As the railroad system became adjusted to the extent that more trains were put on the road, the operation became harassed by the notorious outlaw and train robber, "Railroad Bill." He was a shrewd hombre; in fact his skill in eluding capture was so perfect that the superstitious people around here credited him with being able to disappear or change to an animal upon his desire to do so, when he became cornered by the law. The railroad companies, as well as local merchants and citizens offered great rewards for his capture "Dead or Alive," but this didn't stop these daring raids on the railroads.[1]

Railroad Bill's first documented crime resulted from a law passed by Florida's legislature in 1893 which required that one obtain a license to carry "in his manual possession such Winchester rifle or other repeating rifle." To obtain a license, a person had to post a one-hundred-dollar bond. To break this law was a misdemeanor punishable by fines "not exceeding one hundred dollars or imprisonment in the county jail not exceeding sixty days."[2] Sheriff George E. Smith of Escambia County, Florida, demonstrated the effect of the law in an arrest near Pensacola:

> Sheriff Smith has arrested Ike Harrison, a negro, who says that he has been roaming over the State, carrying a Winchester rifle. He could not give an intelligent account of himself, and was placed in jail to be tried for carrying a Winchester rifle without having given the bond required by law.
>
> *Daily Florida Citizen*, August 16, 1895

Smith's deputy, Allen Brewton, met with different results when he attempted to arrest Railroad Bill at Bluff Springs for carrying a repeating rifle, apparently in the early summer of 1894. According to Robert Brooks, "Deputy Brewton made the mistake of only having a double barrel shotgun when he tried to make the arrest." The problem confronting Brewton was that the effective range of his shotgun was significantly less than that of Railroad Bill's rifle. Thus, the turpentine worker could remain out of Brewton's reach and deliver deadly fire on the officer, who was forced to take "refuge behind a tree."[3]

Hal Cowart, a bystander with a rifle, saw Brewton's predicament and fired on Railroad Bill, allowing the deputy to escape. Cowart probably wasn't firing warning shots. He had killed John Weeks, an African American, at Bluff Springs in 1891 "in a discussion over politics."[4]

The gunfight with Deputy Brewton made Railroad Bill a wanted man in Florida. According to Brooks, after the incident the turpentine employee moved to Teaspoon, a few miles north of Bluff Springs, where "no white person lived." And within months the individual became known to the L&N for "boarding the freight trains alone, breaking into the boxcars and throwing the goods out for his men to collect." He also "fired upon the trainmen several times, and it became dangerous to the trainmen to show themselves in that locality, for fear of being made the target of his Winchester."[5]

L&N detective John B. Harlan wrote a magazine article about the outlaw in 1927. By that time he was L&N's chief of police and probably had access to relevant documents, yet he made numerous errors indicative of someone relying on memory. For example, he incorrectly noted the caliber of Railroad Bill's weapons, the name of Bluff Springs, and the year the outlaw was killed. He stated that Railroad Bill "had shot at several of the trainmen in the territory but without wounding anyone"—apparently forgetting that the desperado was credited with wounding two L&N brakemen. He also stated that the first problem the company encountered with Railroad Bill was in 1894 when he threatened a section foreman on L&N's Pensacola and Atlantic Division's line, which runs from Flomaton to Pensacola. Railroad Bill, however, was not noted in the press for committing a serious crime on that line. Harlan was probably remembering an 1894 incident involving a section foreman at Grand Bay, on the Mobile and New Orleans Division's line, twenty-five miles west of Mobile. It was the most violent threat made against an L&N section foreman that year and possibly for many other years as well.[6]

The incident began on August 12, 1894, after an African

American woman walked several miles from her home to meet a friend arriving by train at Grand Bay. After the woman arrived at the station, she began to quarrel with section foreman W. T. Moabley's young son, who apparently lived in a section house. Section houses were commonly built next to railway stations to house railroad employees. "Her conduct," Moabley said, "became so disorderly that he ordered her off his place and told her that if she came again to his house acting in the manner she had he would thrash her."[7]

When the woman's friend arrived by train, they left the station, and Moabley thought little more of the confrontation until the next day when he was working on a railroad switch with his section crew and road supervisor J. C. Flora. A man approached and said, "I want to see you."[8]

"All right," Moabley replied.

"I understand that you said that you would whip my wife if she came on your place again."

"Yes, I said so."

"Well, whip me first."

Moabley stepped forward. As he did, the man pulled out a .44-caliber revolver and fired twice. "Moabley held his left hand near his breast and the first ball raised the skin on the middle finger. The second ball struck him in the leg and staggered him." The gunman then turned on Flora and fired another shot, which missed and hit Mike (Tillie) Madison, an elderly African American working in Moabley's crew. The bullet passed through Madison's left arm and lodged in his side.[9]

The man fired two more bullets at Moabley. One missed, but the other struck the foreman's thigh a second time, apparently causing him to fall. Then the man placed the muzzle to Moabley's head and pulled the trigger. But the revolver was out of ammunition and failed to fire. Thus, having an empty weapon and facing a strong section crew, the man ran into a nearby swamp. A posse of about a dozen men followed but was unable to apprehend him.[10]

The wounded men were taken to Mobile and attended by Chief Surgeon Rhett Goode. After receiving treatment, Madison went to his home near Magnolia Cemetery in the city, and Moabley went to the depot to catch the evening train back to Grand Bay. A reporter commented that "no one would have thought, from [Moabley's] quiet demeanor, that he had just escaped death or that he had in his pocket two leaden pellets freshly cut from his body."[11]

The shooter was identified as Wash Jackson. Two weeks later, Mobile County sheriff Phelan B. Dorlan and deputy sheriff Frank Cazalas arrested a suspect at the corner of George and Elmira Streets in Mobile who fit the description of Jackson and had Jackson's children with him. The man, nevertheless, claimed to be Tom Jackson, Wash Jackson's brother. Authorities conferred with Wiley Humphries, who had known Jackson for eight years, and Humphries said that Wash did not have a brother. But when Humphries interviewed the prisoner in jail, he confirmed that the suspect was not Wash, even though he "bore a strong resemblance to the man wanted, and had the children of Wash with him, and had rented a house in town to live."[12]

Wash Jackson was still on the lam. That led Sheriff Dorlan to believe that the fugitive had become involved in another violent railroad incident about a week after the Grand Bay assault. The new incident occurred at Hurricane Bayou, and a brakeman had been wounded. Trouble started when L&N conductor Elmer Markle and his crew observed Railroad Bill boarding their train while it was stopped at a station in Baldwin County. When the train reached Hurricane Bayou, they attempted to capture the individual by locking him in a freight car. Railroad Bill, however, somehow escaped and shot brakeman J. C. Williams in the knee.[13]

Dorlan had suspected Jackson of wounding Williams, but the culprit was Railroad Bill. Jackson had children in Mobile, whereas no mention was made in the press of Railroad Bill having family in that city. Jackson was "about thirty-five years old" and had a "very black" complexion, while Railroad Bill was "about 28 years" old and had a "very dark brown, ginger cake color." Railroad Bill typically carried a rifle, multiple pistols, and an ammunition belt. If he had gone to Grand Bay to confront Moabley, he would not have run out of ammunition.[14]

On October 27, two weeks after the wounding of Williams, Railroad Bill was involved in another violent altercation at Hurricane Bayou. This time he forced an L&N crew to board their train and pull out of the station. His motive for commandeering the train is unclear, but the crew probably attempted to capture him or interrupted his attempt to breech a car.[15]

The next day another train crew spotted the outlaw, who was becoming well known to trainmen. He was with a white man two miles north of Mobile between One Mile and Three Mile Creeks. Mobile police officers Edward Morris and James Donoghue were dispatched to investigate. In the reported area, they found a suspicious white man who "gave evasive answers as to the whereabouts of his negro companion." Also, they found two black men hiding in tall grass nearby. The three men "were arrested as dangerous and suspicious characters." One of the African Americans was almost six feet tall, had a smooth face, and bore a scar on his forehead. He claimed to be

Andrew Bright from Atlanta, but he admitted to having been at Hurricane Bayou on the night the train was commandeered. Authorities suspected that he was the assailant and held him until the train crew could return to Mobile to see if they could identify him. Bright, however, was not Railroad Bill.[16]

Railroad Bill was reportedly implicated in another violent incident three months later. On January 26, 1895, Freight Train Number 74 pulled out of Hurricane Bayou at 7:00 p.m. with thirteen black and white tramps riding on a flatcar. By the time the train passed Bay Minette, some of the men had moved to a gondola coal car. Brakemen Robert Stewart and Oscar Wright confronted the men in an attempt to protect the coal, a commodity often pilfered from the railroad and used or sold.[17]

Pistol drawn, Stewart commanded the men to hold up their hands. Everyone obeyed except one black man and one white man, who answered with "a perfect fusillade." One bullet passed through Stewart's shirt, narrowly missing his chest; another struck his right hand, mangling his finger and rendering his pistol inoperable. Meanwhile, another man grabbed Wright, took his pistol, and threw him off the moving train.[18]

The conductor heard the gunshots and ordered the train to stop at Dyas Creek Tank, a few miles east of Bay Minette. As it slowed, the tramps jumped off and disappeared into the woods. A group of five told the others that they were going toward Williams Station to find a dirt road that would take them to Pensacola. "They swore they would die before they would submit to arrest."[19]

Stewart was transported to Mobile and attended by Dr. Goode, who amputated the third finger on the brakeman's right hand. Wright, however, was unhurt and walked to the

Bay Minette Station and notified authorities. Morgan Ashe, a railroad engineer at Bay Minette who often served as a deputy sheriff, formed a posse consisting of Robert Wilking (probably Wilkins), Guy Cain, and James Stewart. They traveled to Dyas Creek and arrested five men, some of whom "confessed to having been on the coal car, when the shooting took place." On one of the men the posse found a pistol that had been taken from a brakeman in a fight with tramps a few days earlier. The men were accompanied to jail at Bay Minette while Ashe, Cain, and Stewart searched for other suspects. Eventually they crossed the state line into Florida.[20]

About 3:30 p.m. on the day after the shooting, the posse came upon five men near Pineville, Florida. Ashe commanded the suspects to halt, but they fired on the posse and a gunfight erupted with the fugitives using revolvers and the posse using rifles. Three black men were captured, while two white men found shelter behind a nearby cabin. As the posse approached the cabin, the white men fled into a nearby swamp. Ashe considered it "impracticable" to pursue, and the posse turned their attention to the prisoners. One was Andrew Jackson of New Iberia, Louisiana, who had been wounded seriously in the back. Another was Louis Ferguson of Birmingham, who had been shot in the thigh near the knee. The third was Oliver Best of Nashville, who was unhurt. Having been captured in Florida, the suspects refused to voluntarily return to Alabama. They were held under guard until an extradition request was approved by the governor's office. Then the men were then taken to Flomaton Station to wait for Passenger Train Number 1 to take them to Mobile. While at the station, Jackson "informed one of the posse that they had formed a plan to wreck the cannon ball train at Bay Minette Saturday night." Derailing and wrecking a train was sometimes a means of robbing it.[21]

Ashe's plan was to take the prisoners to Mobile by train, rest, and then take them by boat across Mobile Bay and place them in jail at Daphne, the seat of Baldwin County. At Mobile, Jackson and Ferguson were admitted to the city hospital while Best was locked in the city jail. Captain Peter Burke, Mobile's chief of police, sent a letter to L&N attorney G. L. Smith, "notifying him that the wounded men were received at the hospital under protest and that the city will submit a bill to the railroad company for expense of caring for them." Burke also interrogated Best and received a signed confession outlining the events that led to the prisoner's arrest. Best confirmed that Ferguson was the man who grabbed Wright, took his pistol, and threw him from the train. Ferguson still had Wright's pistol when he was captured.[22]

Ashe transferred Best to Daphne, but when he returned he learned that Ferguson was improving in the hospital. Jackson, however, had died that morning. Before leaving for Daphne with Ferguson, Ashe stated that he intended to return to Bay Minette and form another posse to search for the two white men who had escaped in Florida.[23]

According to the signed statement Best gave to Burke, thirteen men had boarded the train at Hurricane Bayou. From accounts in the press, five were arrested in Alabama, three were arrested in Florida, and two escaped in Florida. That left three men unaccounted for. One of those may have been Railroad Bill, since reports would eventually attribute Robert Stewart's wounding to him.[24]

About six weeks after the Stewart and Wright incident, Freight Train Number 17, bound for Mobile, pulled up to the water tank at Hurricane Bayou. It was 8:30 a.m., March 6, 1895. The train had orders to wait for Freight Train Number 72 from Mobile to pass. On board were engineer Jack Dorsey, conductor A. J. Cammack, fireman Will Wallace, and brakemen N. E. Rowell, G. W. Kent, and J. S. Martin. Martin climbed down from the train, walked behind the pump house, and found a man asleep.[25]

Dorsey called to Cammack, and the crew gathered around the slumbering man. All agreed that he was the person who had wounded brakeman Williams and was wanted by the company. They removed his rifle and a pistol and roused him. But to their surprise, he bounded to his feet and ran about a hundred yards with them shouting for him to stop. He then pulled a pistol from his shirt and engaged the men in a gunfight. One of the crewmen used Railroad Bill's rifle, which Cammack described as having a stock that looked as if it had been "hewed out" with a hatchet. Cammack also said the outlaw "must have fixed the rifle in some way, for though one of the brakemen took deliberate aim at him it seemed impossible to hit him."[26]

The crew ran low on ammunition and retreated to Mrs. Miller's section house, which she probably operated as a boardinghouse for railroad employees. From there the battle continued. The trainmen called to a telegraph operator named Bryan, who was inside the depot, apparently wanting him to go to his office and send a message for help. But when Bryan stepped out of the depot, Railroad Bill fired, forcing him back inside. Meanwhile, the men had armed themselves with shotguns and shells and were reinforced by members of a railroad bridge crew. According to Cammack, they started out "to get him."[27]

Railroad Bill was heavily outnumbered and outgunned. He was facing death. But just at that moment, Train Number 72 pulled up, and the outlaw climbed into the cab of the locomotive and covered engineer Edward B. Mershon with a revolver. He ordered Mershon to pull past the section house, and as they passed slowly he used Mershon as a shield and "filled the house with lead." The trainmen could not return fire, fearing they would hit the engineer.[28]

Having miraculously escaped death and having a train at his disposal, one might think Railroad Bill would have commanded Mershon to run the engine at full speed to safety. Instead, after only a short distance, he jumped off and took a new position near the telegraph office. That prevented Bryan from returning to the office to send a telegram for help. But when the trainmen saw Railroad Bill's move, they renewed their attack, eventually forcing him to retreat into a nearby swamp. Cammack later commented, "I think I wounded him with a load of buckshot, as he disappeared after that shot."[29]

Kent would comment, "I think a man is justified in killing a desperate character like that." He added that he "shot to kill each time, but [Railroad Bill] seemed to bear a charmed life."[30]

Railroad Bill had escaped death but not injury. Mershon noted that the outlaw was bloody when inside the cab of his locomotive. Also, several African Americans who came to the station after the gunfight said "they had been frightened by the desperado who, when meeting them on the road, had drawn a revolver and demanded of them to hold up their hands and pass on. They noticed that he was bleeding profusely."[31]

The office of the Mobile and Montgomery Division in Montgomery issued an explanation:

During the past year many freight cars have been broken into and robbed while en route between Flomaton and Mobile, and the railroad authorities fixed the robberies on a party of some half a dozen negroes, who had as their leader a big, black fellow calling himself "Railroad." His real name has never been ascertained, and all that is known of him evolved out of the several nervy robberies which he directed. "Railroad" and his gang of thieves seem to have had their headquarters in the wilds of Baldwin county between Mobile and Flomaton Junction.

Montgomery *Daily Advertiser*, March 7, 1895

Morgan Ashe formed a posse after the Hurricane Bayou gunfight and searched for the assailant. Railroad Bill, however, apparently did not leave a trail that was easily followed: "A boat that had been chained to the river bank was found missing and the lock broken, and from this it was surmised that Bill had gone down the river and taken to the swamp." Ashe's posse continued to search for several days, crossing into Florida where Ashe had lost the two white men after the Stewart and Wright incident. But when they reached Bluff Springs, Ashe was handed a telegram stating that the desperado was back in Baldwin County.[32]

A section foreman and a brakeman on a southbound train had seen Railroad Bill, "heavily armed," at the water tank at Hurricane Bayou at 6:00 a.m. on Saturday, March 9. From there he went to the Phillips farmhouse, and afterward he went with an accomplice to the Williamson farmhouse, looking for a rifle to replace the one he lost in the gunfight. He and the accomplice then went to the Perdido water tank and found Green Richardson, a young African American, in charge. Railroad Bill told Richardson that he was looking for Cammack, Kent, and Nat Crosby, the trainmen he had fought at Hurricane Bayou.

Richardson said the men had been transferred to the north end of the road.[33]

"Well, I'll go to the north end after them," Railroad Bill said. "I'm after them—especially Crosby. He's the one who shot me."[34]

7

Gunfight at Stewart's Barn

A few days after Railroad Bill threatened the trainmen he fought at Hurricane Bayou, he was spotted with fifteen to eighteen tramps at Dyas Creek Tank. A posse responded from Bay Minette, arriving about sundown and searching until midnight without success. The only serious criminal incident that night was covered by the Montgomery *Daily Advertiser*: "Conductor William Neighbors reported that while on his freight train at Williams Station he was fired on by a negro—a black negro evidently not 'Railroad.'"[1]

Little information was published regarding the whereabouts of Railroad Bill for about a month. Then on Saturday, April 6, 1895, he reappeared in a momentous way at 9:30 p.m. on a wagon road about half a mile south of Bay Minette. In the dark he happened upon Calvin A. Stapleton and Robert Wilkins.[2]

"Hello, is that you John?" asked Railroad Bill.

"No," replied Wilkins.[3]

The outlaw trailed them for a few steps. Then Wilkins stopped and ordered him "in pretty strong language, to quit following them." Railroad Bill responded by crouching behind a tree and opening fire. One bullet passed through Stapleton's right thigh; another grazed Wilkins's coat. Stapleton was unarmed, but Wilkins returned fire, emptying his revolver at their assailant. The men then ran to Bay Minette, knowing that they had just escaped "the notorious desperado and car thief, Railroad Bill."[4]

Wilkins found Detective Thomas Watts talking with Morgan Ashe at the railroad station and exclaimed that he had just dueled with Railroad Bill. "This was incredible," Watts said. "I thought Wilkins was joking, but it was no joke."[5]

Watts had learned in his investigations of Railroad Bill that several people living near Bay Minette had been harboring the outlaw. One of them was Emma Davis, whom Watts described as "'Railroad's' particular friend." She had recently ordered a large quantity of Winchester cartridges in Mobile, and the ammunition had been delivered to her in Bay Minette that day. Watts believed the cartridges were intended for the outlaw and thought that he would not be long in calling for them. He also knew that Railroad Bill sometimes boarded eastbound Freight Train Number 74 at night as it slowed on a steep grade two miles west of Bay Minette. Believing Railroad Bill might board the train that night to get to Davis, Watts decided to try to intercept him. The detective caught the train in Mobile, and when it reached Hurricane Bayou he climbed on a catwalk above a freight car to watch for the desperado. When the train arrived at Bay Minette without incident, he got off to talk with Ashe, whom he had telegraphed to meet him.[6]

Watts asked Morgan Ashe, James H. Stewart (Robert Stewart's brother), and seventeen-year-old Fred Wilkins to go with him to search for Railroad Bill that night. The elderly Stapleton, who had been wounded, protested the plan; nevertheless, he loaned Watts a shotgun to use in addition to three large revolvers the detective was carrying. The posse's search took them about eight miles south of town.[7]

Watts recalled that the "tramp through blind roads leading through heavily timbered swamps where the night was as dark as pitch, expecting every minute to hear the crack of Railroad's rifle and hear the disagreeable song of bullets, was one that I shall never forget." The men stopped at the cabins of several African Americans before arriving at the old homestead of Mr. and Mrs. Lane Stewart, parents of James and Robert Stewart. The vacant house with broken windowpanes was situated on the crest of a hill. Silhouetted against the moonlit sky, it reminded Watts of a haunted house. Carefully, the posse peered through the windows, but no one was inside.[8] Watts said:

> We decided to visit the barn which is a rickety old-fashioned shed affair that has a wagon way running through the center, a hay loft above and stables on both sides.
>
> Just as we were about to enter a stall door a scraping noise was heard. Morgan Ashe thought it had been made by pigs and was about to enter when I held him back, and in a few seconds the unmistakable sound of a Winchester breech being opened, warned us that our game was at hand. "Railroad" sung out, "What do you all want around here?" He was commanded to come out, but refused with a lot of oaths.
>
> Montgomery *Daily Advertiser*, March 8, 1896

The posse decided to keep the outlaw in the barn until he ran out of ammunition or until it became morning.[9] According to Watts:

> We all hunted trees in a minute, Ashe and Wilkins finding splendid protection behind two big oaks in front of the barn; Stewart found one near the rear corner on one side, and I got on the other, opposite the point where "Railroad's" voice was heard.
>
> My breast-works was a mulberry tree shaped like an "S," and affording very little protection, and I hadn't been behind it more than a second before I saw the muzzle of "Railroad's" rifle shoved out one of the big openings between the plank sides of the stable. That gun looked like one of those cannon you see sticking out of the sides of the cruiser Montgomery, and it was not but a few feet away, too.
>
> Montgomery *Daily Advertiser*, March 8, 1896

Railroad Bill could see the men in the moonlight, but they could not see him inside the barn. His shots, however, could be "traced from one end of the barn to the other by the flashes from his gun."[10] Watts continued:

> Railroad's first shot cracked at me and the bullet grazed over my left ear, through my hair and cut through my hat band.
>
> I could not see him, but as soon as he fired I blazed away with a load of buckshot at the spot where his powder exploded, and in a few minutes he came back at me from a point several feet away, having withdrawn his gun and stuck it out though another crack.

It became entirely too hot behind the mulberry tree, so I dropped back into the shade of a peach tree, but his fire followed me, one ball grazing my side and going through my coat-tails. In the meanwhile I had shot twenty times and had to reload to do so. I shifted my position by running around to the vacant house and entering a room not many feet away from the barn.

There were two windows in the room and I fired first from one and then from the other, and "Railroad" continued to blaze away at me. We were both playing the same dodge game, and all this time Ashe, Wilkins and Stewart were firing into the barn, but their positions put them out of his reach.

Montgomery Daily Advertiser, March 8, 1896

The fight occurred near midnight, and about fifty shots were exchanged, making the barn "a perfect sieve." A silence followed that was longer than Railroad Bill needed to reload. Watts then heard two more shots from Stewart's position. Those were followed by a whistle, making Watts hope "that they had killed the bird."[11] He described what occurred next:

Running around the barn I heard a stifled groan and lying face downward, his head buried in the plowed ground; his rifle clinched in his hands and thrown out in front of him. Stewart was dead.

Evidently "Railroad" made a bold dash for liberty carrying his gun ready to shoot while on the run. Stewart saw him coming and stepped out to kill him, but the negro was too quick; his shot was fatal; Stewart's went wild [*sic*] of the mark.

Montgomery Daily Advertiser, March 8, 1896

Stewart was thirty years old and "died within thirty feet of where he had been born."[12] But there was an even more unsettling aspect of his death:

> Speaking of a man "biting the dust" when killed, there was an impressive coincidence about this expression in the murder of Young Stewart. Before starting out on the hunt after Slater, Watts, Stewart, Ashe and Wilkins held a consultation and in planning their line of action it was agreed that if one man got killed the others would stand until all met death if necessary. "Well, I'll hold up my end," said Stewart. "If we catch the black devil I'll stay with him until one of us bites the dust." This was prophetic: When Stewart fell forward pierced through the heart by the bullet from "Railroad's" rifle, his face buried itself in the plowed earth and when his body was picked up, the comrades of the dead man found his mouth filled with dirt.
>
> Montgomery *Daily Advertiser*, April 10, 1895

Ashe returned to Bay Minette and sent a telegram to Escambia County sheriff Edward S. McMillan. The sheriff arrived from Brewton at 5:00 a.m. on a train with several bloodhounds. Ashe led him to the barn, and the dogs picked up Railroad Bill's scent. They followed it for about two miles before losing it in heavy rain.[13]

Alabama governor William C. Oates authorized a reward of $150 for Railroad Bill's apprehension. The money would be paid in addition to $350 being offered by the L&N. The Atlanta *Constitution* commented that "$500 is sufficient to justify an enterprising officer in hunting him down."[14]

8

The Death of Mark Stinson

The L&N hired informants to provide information on the whereabouts and plans of Railroad Bill. Detective John Harlan discussed their strategy when writing about the desperado in an article in the *L&N Employes' Magazine*:

> Several negro detectives were employed to "get in" or to associate with him, but they were never able to gain "Railroad Bill's" confidence. While he would treat them kindly, he always acted in a way that would satisfy them that he was more or less suspicious and they were never able to accomplish the ends for which they had been employed.[1]

Mark M. Stinson would become the exception. After Stinson was observed with the outlaw on several occasions, railroad detectives attempted to recruit him as an informant. But according to the Montgomery *Daily Advertiser*, "it was an impossibility to catch him," since he was as wary as Railroad Bill. A woman named Susan Austin would recruit Stinson. She lived near Pollard, Alabama, and sometimes she cooked for the James McMillan family. James was Sheriff Edward McMillan's older brother and had served as sheriff before Edward. Austin told him she wanted to help in capturing Railroad Bill, and James arranged for her to meet with railroad officials. They assigned her the task of recruiting Stinson. It took her about a month (apparently late September 1894), then she sent a telegram to L&N officials stating that she and Stinson would endeavor to capture the outlaw. The station agent at Bay Minette, J. F. Cooper, became Stinson's contact within the company. Stinson, however, distrusted L&N officials and only sent letters to Cooper. In one he stated that he was attempting to persuade Railroad Bill to surrender. In another he asked Cooper to send a letter to Perdido that he could collect the next day. It probably contained his pay.[2]

The L&N had not been taking threats from Railroad Bill lightly:

> "This man Salters [Railroad Bill] is really a dangerous character as you will readily believe," said a railroad official. "The operations of his gang of freight car robbers have extended over a period of a year or more, and they have stolen lots of goods. The leader is absolutely fearless and desperately bold, and now that he has it in for the trainmen for having wounded him, killed one of his partners [Andrew Jackson] and jailed another [Louis Ferguson], he is intent upon evening up scores."
>
> Montgomery *Daily Advertiser*, March 12, 1895

Not only had Railroad Bill threatened the crewmen he fought at Hurricane Bayou, but he had threatened to kill Superintendent McKinney. That threat apparently encouraged McKinney to negotiate a deal with Stinson to betray and capture the outlaw. McKinney traveled 142 miles from his office in Montgomery to intercept Stinson when he appeared for his letter in Perdido. Stinson, however, did not call for the letter, so McKinney traveled to Mobile to spend the night. The next morning he returned on a fast freight train but arrived too late. Stinson had retrieved the letter and disappeared about half an hour earlier.[3]

McKinney boarded a slow freight train back to Montgomery. But when he was about two miles northeast of Perdido, near Sullivan's Switch and Wilson Station, he saw Stinson standing in the doorway of a cabin. It was the residence of Henry and Mary Caldwell. Detective Harlan described Henry as "a partner who traveled with [Railroad Bill] as a kind of assistant." McKinney jumped off the train, returned through the woods to Perdido, and directed station agent R. L. Stewart—who had probably given Stinson the letter—to go to the cabin and ask the undercover informant for a meeting. Stewart did as directed, but Mary said Stinson had left.[4]

McKinney did not believe Mary and sent Stewart back to the cabin to watch for Stinson. Eventually he appeared, and Stewart approached him with McKinney's request. Stinson "seemed afraid" when Stewart stated that McKinney wanted to talk with him. But when Stewart assured him that the superintendent did not wish to arrest him, Stinson agreed to meet McKinney the next morning.[5] The conference took place in a swamp near Wilson Station:

> [Stinson] was standing with his hand on a murderous looking knife sticking in unpleasant suggestiveness in his belt, while his other hand was back on his hip pocket. The

Superintendent walked up to him as unconcernedly as possible under the circumstances, and assured him that he had no idea of trying to arrest him—that as Railroad had spread it broadcast that he intended to kill him on sight, he thought it his duty to get him if possible.

Montgomery *Daily Advertiser*, March 8, 1896

A few nights later, Stinson met with Cooper at the Bay Minette Station and agreed to meet with McKinney the next night. The superintendent traveled to Bay Minette but was delayed and arrived too late. Stinson, nevertheless, had promised to return a few nights later. For that meeting McKinney went to the dispatcher's office in Montgomery so that he could communicate by telegraph with Stinson and Cooper at Bay Minette. In that conference, Stinson and McKinney agreed to meet again face-to-face a few nights later. But as Cooper watched Stinson leave the station after the telegraphic conference, he observed that Stinson gave "a low whistle and was joined by another negro who was waiting behind a pile of cross ties about 100 yards down the track."

McKinney interpreted that as "foul play" and arranged for security before the next meeting. He stationed Detective Watts, Robert Wilkins, and J. F. Goodson around the meeting site to make sure Stinson came by himself. Indeed, Stinson arrived alone and assured McKinney that he "would do what he had promised."[6]

What could Stinson have promised that was important enough for McKinney, a railroad executive, to travel from Montgomery on multiple occasions to negotiate? The Montgomery *Daily Advertiser* stated that McKinney offered the undercover agent all the reward money if he would capture

Railroad Bill. But that was not a novel offer. It already existed for anyone willing to bring Railroad Bill to justice or to the undertaker's office. Based on events that would transpire at Mount Vernon in April 1895, a village twenty-nine miles north of Mobile, it would seem that McKinney offered Stinson a negotiated amount for setting up Railroad Bill so that L&N detectives could capture the notorious outlaw. Understandably, Stinson may not have wanted to personally apprehend the man who had befriended him. But such an offer by McKinney would allow the undercover agent to receive a handsome sum without having to make the capture.

Stinson's opportunity apparently did not mature until early April 1895, when Henry Caldwell was arrested and sentenced to hard labor in Escambia County, Alabama, for robbing the contents of freight cars. Stinson then replaced Caldwell as Railroad Bill's lieutenant, and Stinson seems to have lost little time in attempting to fulfill his promise to McKinney. Evidently, that promise was to lure Railroad Bill to a predetermined destination so that railroad detectives could make their capture. The scheme, however, would cost Stinson his life.[7]

Stinson would mysteriously disappear in mid-April 1895, and his fate was unknown until 1898 when fishermen accidentally raised his remains in their net from a lagoon. His body had been weighted and dumped into a waterway. It is unclear which lagoon held Stinson's remains, but it was probably near the outskirts of Mount Vernon, the last known location of the informant. "The general supposition," according to Detective Harlan, "is that 'Railroad Bill' killed him and did away with the body." But why would the outlaw, who was already wanted for murder, take the time and effort to transport, weight, and sink the body of an informant so that it could not be found?

Wouldn't it have made more sense to leave it as a sign to others who might consider cooperating with the law?[8]

The story of Stinson's demise began on April 12, 1895—six days after Railroad Bill killed James Stewart. Detectives tracked Railroad Bill to Pollard and "had him caged in the vicinity of Pollard Station." But for some reason they did not attempt an arrest. That night he "broke into the armory of the Pollard military company and stole several rifles and a big lot of ammunition."[9]

The robbery was evidently to raise cash, since Railroad Bill was observed with "a big roll of money" the next day. Moreover, the stolen rifles and ammunition were not suitable for his personal use. The standard military-issued rifle was the .45-caliber trapdoor Springfield. The military had begun to replace it with an improved weapon in 1892, but most military units, and essentially all state militia units, still carried the trapdoor. It used a large cartridge and was renowned for accuracy, but the user had to insert a new cartridge manually before each shot. In contrast, the Winchester rifle used a smaller, less powerful cartridge, but the user could fire it rapidly by operating a lever between shots. It became renowned as "The Gun That Won the West."[10]

Railroad Bill must have had assistance in the armory robbery as well as a ready market for the rifles and most of the ammunition. The weight and bulk of the munitions would have been difficult for one person to transport very far on foot. Moreover, after spending the night "under a lumber shed on a farm near the village," he traveled to Stockton, probably by taking a train from Pollard to Bay Minette and then walking ten miles northward. At Stockton he engaged Wesley Smith, an African American with a bateau, to paddle him across the

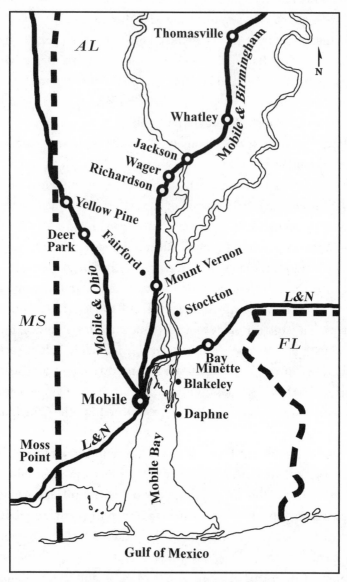

Region of the Mount Vernon manhunt for Railroad Bill.

waterways of the Mobile-Tensaw River delta and land him at Mount Vernon Ferry.[11]

Railroad detectives followed the outlaw and interviewed Smith at Stockton. The boatman said his passenger had a wad of cash, carried a Winchester and a large cavalry pistol, and was "dressed in blue pantaloons, a heavy blue flannel shirt, black vest and no coat." He also said that Railroad Bill "walked as though his feet were paining him" and carried "a greasy leather ammunition sack" suspended by a leather belt over his shoulder. The sack probably contained cartridges from the armory. The weight of the load might explain his sore feet if he walked from Bay Minette.[12]

But why would Railroad Bill bring cartridges that he could not use in any of his weapons? Possibly he intended to sell them at Mount Vernon. The village had a decades-long history as a military outpost and arsenal. It was at Mount Vernon that the U.S. Army held Geronimo and a small band of Apaches as prisoners of war for seven years, allowing them to camp around the barracks before they were transported to Fort Sill, Oklahoma, in 1894. Years of military presence had probably given rise to an underground market for trapdoor ammunition pilfered from the army.[13]

Stinson, who may have been with Railroad Bill at Pollard, also came to Mount Vernon, but not with the desperado. He would likely have taken the conventional route: an L&N train to Mobile, followed by a Mobile and Birmingham Railroad train to Mount Vernon. Since that route required a transfer between railroad companies in the city, Railroad Bill would have avoided it to prevent being recognized.

Somehow railroad detectives had effectively tracked Railroad Bill to Pollard and then to Stockton, probably with information from Stinson or Austin. For certain, only Stinson or Austin could have provided the next piece of information: where Railroad Bill would be on the night of April 15. The detectives knew he would be on the outskirts of Mount Vernon in an obscure cabin by the Mobile and Birmingham Railroad track. There they planned to capture him about midnight.

Two posses were assembled for the Mount Vernon manhunt. One was a sheriffs' posse composed of Sheriff Edward McMillan with Deputies Wilkins and Burrows of Escambia County, and Sheriff Phelan B. Dorlan with Deputies Charles Murphy and Frank Cazalas of Mobile County. A second posse assembled was a detectives' posse led by L&N chief detective C. M. Warner from headquarters in Louisville. He was assisted by Detectives Williams, Watts, Suggs, and Burrows and by two African Americans.[14]

Newspapermen in Mobile apparently observed both posses in the city on Monday, April 15, and knew their objective was to capture Railroad Bill at Mount Vernon. In the afternoon the sheriffs' posse left the city on a Mobile and Birmingham Railroad train. After passing through Mount Vernon, they arrived at Richardson, twenty-four miles farther north. They ate supper and walked to a nearby trestle to make camp. By checking trains and watching the trestle, they could intercept Railroad Bill if he fled northward from Mount Vernon.[15]

After the sheriffs' posse had left Mobile, the detectives' posse, "armed with Winchesters, revolvers and countless rounds of ammunition," traveled by special engine to Mount Vernon, arriving at 8:00 p.m. Their presence was no surprise to villagers, who had probably learned of their plan from reporters in Mobile. But by then their manhunt had developed additional complications. Railroad Bill did not go directly to the cabin after being landed at Mount Vernon Ferry on Sunday. Instead, he happened upon an elderly African American named Mary Jane Samuels and presented himself as a hunter "whose feet had given out." Seeing that his feet "were blistered so that he could hardly walk," she agreed to let him stay at her house, and he paid her in advance for three days' room and board.[16]

The next day, Monday morning, Railroad Bill locked his Winchester and ammunition in Mary Jane's wardrobe and proceeded to purchase meat and provisions from one of the principal stores in town, which was owned by James DuCloux. Inside the store, he was surprised to find men discussing him and the posses which would arrive that evening to capture him. As the men talked about joining a posse to share in the reward money, Railroad Bill boldly entered their discussion. A detective would later comment that the outlaw "was smart enough and had the nerve to join in the conversation, allaying suspicion as to his identify by giving a very open-faced and highly plausible account of himself."[17]

Railroad Bill returned to Mary Jane's home, retrieved his rifle and ammunition, and said he was going hunting. He did not, however, flee, as one might expect of someone with two posses bearing down on him. Instead, he returned to Mary Jane's home with a rabbit that he had killed, ate supper, and left again, this time telling her that he was "going out to see some of the boys." She never saw him again.[18]

That night in Mobile, reporters waited for news from the Mount Vernon manhunt. A telegram arrived at 1:00 a.m. Tuesday stating that "Bill had been surrounded in a house near the river and a battle followed, resulting in the death of the negro." It was sensational news, and at least one newspaper carried it in a morning edition. Later, however, the revelation had to be retracted: Railroad Bill was not dead. When Superintendent McKinney was asked about the false report, he answered, "I only wish this story were true."[19]

Later in the day, the detectives found and interviewed Mary Jane Samuels at her home. For breakfast, she had cooked the rabbit that Railroad Bill had killed. (One of the detectives later commented that the desperado had shot it "square through the back with his rifle, which proves his ability as a marksman.") After the interview, Mary Jane was "sure that her self-made guest was none other than he, whose scalp is worth $500 to the man that secures it."[20]

About the time Mary Jane was interviewed, the leaders in the detectives' posse—Warner, Williams, and Watts—left Mount Vernon for Montgomery. Only Watts was expected to return to the remaining men. The move seems perplexing, particularly with the posse close on Railroad Bill's trail.[21]

The departure of Warner, Williams, and Watts apparently resulted from events that had transpired at the cabin. The first report at 1:00 a.m. stated that Railroad Bill was killed in a gunfight. That news was corrected by the following account:

> The posse was informed that the desperado had fortified himself in a shanty near the railroad, which he was reported to have stocked with a quantity of ammunition and provisions, as if he expected to withstand a siege. The posse repaired to the shanty indicated and after calling on the negro to surrender and receiving no response, opened fire on what they supposed was the negro's stronghold; after riddling the old hut with bullets and there still being no signs of life about the hut a reconnaissance was determined upon. Under cover of the darkness several

of the party crawled up to the hut only to discover that the bird had flown, and that they had wasted a lot of ammunition for nothing. It was subsequently learned that the negro had received a tip that the posse was after him and had skipped about three-quarters of an hour before the posse arrived.

Mobile *Daily Register*, April 18, 1895

The above might be believable if it wasn't contradicted by a subsequent and significantly different account. That account stated that "we arrived at Mount Vernon and located the house in which 'Railroad' had been lying out. One of our men secreted himself in the house, but the bird came not back. He had flown." Thus, the posse's story had shifted from the outlaw being killed in a gunfight, to an empty cabin having been riddled with bullets, to a posse member being inside the cabin with no mention of gunfire.[22]

But additional contradictions were forthcoming. In an interview with the press, one of the detectives made a seemingly offhand comment to explain the fate of Mark Stinson:

By the by, it is now almost positively established that a dangerous negro named Stinson, who was one of "Railroad's" pals, was killed in the desperate duel in the barn near Bay Minette several nights ago, when young Stewart lost his life at the hands of the desperado. The body of Stinson was carried into an adjacent swamp and buried.

Montgomery *Daily Advertiser*, April 18, 1895

Detective Watts must not have been pleased with the above account, which implicated him in wrongdoing at Stewart's barn. That may have contributed to Warner's attempt then to set the record truthfully in the press without disclosing embarrassing details:

> Chief detective Warner, of the Louisville and Nashville railroad, passed through [Montgomery] last night en route back to Louisville. He did not catch "Railroad Bill" nor kill him, but his posse did succeed in killing a negro named Stinson, a pal of the desperado.
>
> Atlanta *Constitution*, April 19, 1895

A likely scenario of what transpired at the Mount Vernon cabin can be teased from reports issued afterward. It would seem that, in the darkness, the detectives' posse accidentally killed Stinson, mistaking him for Railroad Bill. Hurriedly, they issued the news by telegram before discovering their mistake. Then they weighted and sank the body in a nearby lagoon to hide their blunder, particularly from Superintendent McKinney. They also issued a correction to their earlier report. But then they contradicted the correction with additional accounts. Possibly through Watts, McKinney learned the truth and recalled the leadership to his office at Montgomery to explain how his star informant had been killed and Railroad Bill was still free. In leaving Montgomery, Warner and Williams continued to Louisville, and neither detective would be mentioned again in the press as having participated in subsequent efforts to capture Railroad Bill. Watts, however, returned to the posse on Wednesday, but by then it was too late: Railroad Bill had eluded the sheriffs' posse at Richardson and was fleeing northward toward Selma.

A Montgomery newspaper declared, "Railroad Bill killed Mark Stinson—there is no doubt of that." But this was incorrect. The misconception, nevertheless, continued through the years, leading some to include Stinson's death in computing the number of men that Railroad Bill was thought to have killed.[23]

Stinson's untimely end was revealed in 1898:

> Stinson suddenly disappeared and his whereabouts have never been known until a few days ago when some fishermen in dredging one of the numerous lagoons in that part of the country found part of a human skull—the jawbone—that was known to be Stinson by the reason that none of the teeth were there except two stumps in the center. The unfortunate negro was murdered by Railroad Bill, who had shrewdly gotten on to his little game, and the body sunk with weights in the lagoon. After some scientific begging the skull was secured by Special Agent Bow Lowe, of the L. and N., and it now reposes in a drawer in Superintendent McKinney's office at the Union station.
>
> Brewton *Standard Gauge*, December 29, 1898

Undoubtedly, McKinney knew more about the morbid memento than was ever revealed in the press.

Left: Clara Phillips Wolfe during a 1977 interview at Perdido, Alabama. Courtesy of the Fairhope *Courier*.

Below: Sheriff Edward S. McMillan in 1886. Used with permission of the Ed Leigh McMillan Collection.

Right: The cross worn by Kate Leigh McMillan to the funeral of her husband, Sheriff Edward S. McMillan, after he was killed by Railroad Bill. Used with permission of Allison Sinrod.

Below: Kate Leigh McMillan wearing the cross commemorating the loss of her husband, Sheriff Edward S. McMillan. Used with permission of the Ed Leigh McMillan Collection.

Right: James Leonard McGowin, the man who killed Railroad Bill. Used with permission of the Escambia County (Alabama) Historical Society and Thomas E. McMillan Museum.

Below: The building that housed Tidmore and Ward's store in which Railroad Bill was killed. From the Atmore *Spectrum*, December 5, 1907.

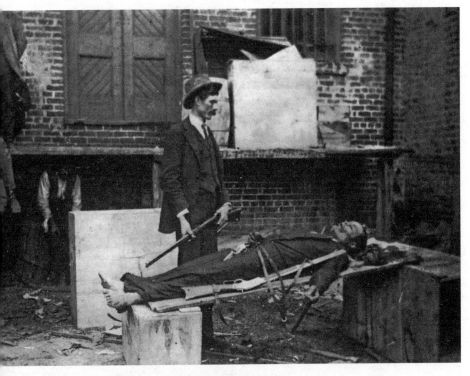

Photograph of Railroad Bill taken shortly after his body was embalmed on March 8, 1896. Used with permission of the Ed Leigh McMillan Collection.

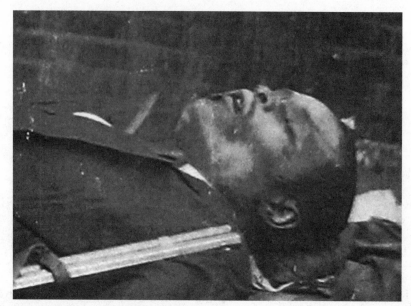

The face of Railroad Bill enlarged from the photograph taken of him in death. Used with permission of the Ed Leigh McMillan Collection.

The handmade shoulder strap and the right hand of Railroad Bill enlarged from the photograph taken of him in death. Used with permission of the Ed Leigh McMillan Collection.

Right: Photograph of A. M. McMillan published with his obituary, May 31, 1896. Used with permission of the Ed Leigh McMillan Collection.

Below: St. John's Cemetery interment card used to record the burial of Railroad Bill, a.k.a. Morris Slater, on March 30, 1896. Used with permission of the Friends of the St. John's Cemetery Foundation.

NAME OF INTERRED	DATE OF INTERMENT
1 Infant Theo Weber	May 21, 1896
2 Hattie Williams	" 19, 1896
3 Charlotte Henderson	" 15, 1896
4 Rhoda Meriwether	" 2, 1896
5 Hiram Fawster	Aprl 21, 1896
6 Susan McLanie	" 18, 1896
7 Christian Stribling	" 13, 1896
8 Morris Slater	Mch 30, 1896
9 Child Spencer Hunter	" 16, 1896
10 Dicyan Berry	Feb 9, 1896

Railroad Bill's headstone in St. John's Cemetery, Pensacola, Florida, which was placed on the grave in 2012 by Margaret G. Massey, wife of the author. Author photo.

First commercial recording of "Railroad Bill," made by Riley Puckett, September 11, 1924. Author photo.

9

The Murder of
Sheriff Edward McMillan

Railroad Bill fled northward, leaving the detectives' posse at Mount Vernon, on Tuesday, April 16, 1895. A freight-train crew saw him in the morning about two miles south of the sheriffs' posse at Richardson. That afternoon he was seen at Wagar, one mile north of Richardson. He had apparently bypassed the sheriffs' posse dressed as a woman, perhaps in clothes from the wardrobe at Mary Jane Samuels's home in which he had locked his rifle and ammunition the previous day.[1]

On Wednesday afternoon Railroad Bill was reported at Whatley, twenty-five miles north of Wagar. When Sheriff Edward McMillan heard the news, he concluded that Railroad Bill was headed to Selma. To head him off, the sheriffs' posse moved up to Thomasville, eighteen miles north of Whatley, and posted guards on the roads and railways. Sheriff Dorlan was confident that they would make an arrest, probably that night. But by Friday it was obvious that the outlaw had eluded them again, and without information such as Mark Stinson had once provided, they had little chance of finding him. Consequently, on Friday afternoon the posse abandoned their effort and boarded a train back to Mobile.[2]

But during the posse's return to the city, a party boarded the train at Mount Vernon and told them that a person matching Railroad Bill's description had been seen getting on a logging train near Fairford, eight miles northwest of Mount Vernon. It was a private railway that ran westward toward Yellow Pine on the Mobile and Ohio Railroad near the Mississippi state line, fifty-nine miles north of Mobile. The suspect was described as having "an oil coat and something wrapped up in it." Sheriff McMillan suspected the coat was wrapped around Railroad Bill's Winchester, giving credence to the report. So when the posse arrived in Mobile, they made preparations to renew their search, but it would be in vain. A newspaper commented, "additional evidence of the foxy cunning, astounding boldness and cool bravery of Morris Slater, alias 'Railroad,' crops out daily."[3] That sentiment was shared by a railroad detective involved in the Mount Vernon manhunt:

> I'll tell you, that negro is the most dangerous and the sharpest I ever came in contact with during a service of many years in the detective business. He has the whole of that section of Alabama terrorized: for the negroes are protecting him, and for that matter he can buy his way through the wild country. Why, within the last few days, he has traveled part of the way disguised as a woman, which demonstrates his cleverness.
>
> Mobile *Daily Register*, April 19, 1895

About a week after the Mount Vernon manhunt ended, a report from Tower in Baldwin County made it seem that the reward money might not be needed:

> "Railroad Bill," the negro desperado and train robber, accompanied by several of his pals, ran upon a camp of white moonshiners engaged in the act of making whisky. The outlaws, who have been pursued for two weeks past by railroad officers, jumped at the conclusion that they had encountered the posse and commenced firing. The moonshiners concluded they were a revenue band and a general fusillade was commenced. "Railroad" was shot six times, the report says, and several of the moonshiners were hit. Several are reported as being fatally wounded, but the survivors on each side bore the injured away and the result is not known.
>
> Atlanta *Constitution*, April 27, 1895

It is unclear if Superintendent McKinney or Sheriff McMillan believed the Tower report, but it became a moot issue early in July when Railroad Bill was reported "beating about between Flomaton, Bluff Springs, Wilson and Bay Minette."[4]

After James Stewart's death, Sheriff Edward McMillan had made Railroad Bill's capture the primary objective of his term in office. According to historian R.L. Scribner, there was a tradition in the McMillan family that Sheriff McMillan vowed to capture or kill Railroad Bill. In return the outlaw sent a note stating, "I wish you hadn't made that statement because I love you, Mr. Ed, and I don't want to kill you."[5]

But Sheriff McMillan came from a family of law officers and was not easily intimidated. His father and his brother James had served as sheriffs of Escambia County, Alabama, and James had left a sterling record. The *Memorial Record of Alabama* described him as "one of the most efficient sheriffs Escambia county has ever had" and as "a terror to all law breakers in Escambia and adjoining counties." It was Scribner's belief that Edward McMillan sought the apprehension of Railroad Bill as a means of surpassing the accomplishments of his brother in office. In any case, after vowing to capture or kill Railroad Bill and then being threatened by the outlaw, the sheriff became entangled in a life-or-death struggle with the desperado.[6]

For some time, Superintendent McKinney—"the man above all others whom [Railroad Bill] wanted to kill"—had been entangled in a similar life-or-death struggle and "sought every means to have [the outlaw] captured or killed." With mutual respect and a shared goal, he and McKinney collaborated and to some extent coordinated their operations. But at every turn their efforts were confounded by "parties who kept [Railroad Bill] posted on the movements of the officers and also kept him supplied with ammunition etc."[7] To counter that advantage, McKinney hired additional informants, two of whom he mentioned in a letter to McMillan on June 28, 1895:

> If you want me to come down any time to assist you I will come.
>
> I sent for Francis Baker and got after for not showing your party where R. R. was: he said that he was in the McDonald house and that he went back there and met him again Monday night. I am inclined to believe he is lying and is afraid of Railroad.
>
> I have stopped his work and thought if I would let him rest awhile we might get something out of him. He says Railroad told [him] he was not going to surrender.

I have not heard a word from Wm Saunders; I sup-
pose by R. R. being down in that vicinity that Saunders
is scared & afraid to have any thing more to do with the
case.

If we do not get him I will try and see if we can get
Baker to locate him that is if your men do not succeed in
running him out. Let me hear from you at any convenient
time.[8]

McMillan spent most of June 1895 away from his office searching for Railroad Bill. Meanwhile, citizens back home planned
an Independence Day celebration to "eclipse all attempts of the
past." Committees were convened to make plans for baseball
games, foot races, bicycle races, shooting contests, barbecues,
basket picnics, and refreshments—free to all. No one could
have guessed that the Fourth of July of 1895 would be "one of
the gloomiest days that was ever spent by Brewtonites."[9]

Sheriff McMillan's vigilance in seeking Railroad Bill's capture was having an effect on the desperado, who began making
overtures to Superintendent McKinney through third parties,
indicating he wanted to surrender:

He was tired of being hounded and wanted to give up if
he could make satisfactory terms. He had a special dislike
for Sheriff McMillan and said that he didn't want him
to have anything to do with his arrest. "Railroad" feared
that he would be mobbed when taken, and that was the
protection he wanted guaranteed before surrendering
himself.

Montgomery *Daily Advertiser*, July 4, 1895

Surrender had been a recurring theme since the days of Stinson, and McKinney ignored such overtures. Besides, he had

not seen anything tangible from Railroad Bill and believed him to be unrepentant. Moreover, Francis Baker, one of the superintendent's undercover informants, had stated that Railroad Bill "was not going to surrender."[10]

Sheriff McMillan's vigilance in southern Alabama seems also to have encouraged Railroad Bill to seek refuge in Florida, outside the sheriff's jurisdiction. On June 30, 1895, he was reported at Molino, twenty-two miles north of Pensacola. Deputy Sheriff A. G. Gordon responded from Pensacola with a posse, but when they arrived they learned that Railroad Bill had moved sixteen miles farther north to Bluff Springs, where he had once lived and where he still had friends to provide assistance.[11]

Probably through officials with the L&N or the Escambia County, Florida, sheriff's office, Sheriff Edward McMillan learned that Railroad Bill was somewhere near Bluff Springs. He then embarked on a plan for Railroad Bill's capture. It resembled the plan employed at Mount Vernon. But rather than railroad detectives attempting to capture the outlaw, McMillan would attempt the job. Deputy Gordon's posse would remain at Molino to block Railroad Bill's escape to the south, while Sheriff McMillan's posse would move down from Alabama to make a capture at Bluff Springs. Having an Alabama sheriff make an arrest in Florida seemed to introduce a legal dilemma, but according to Gould Beech, who conferred with the McMillan family in the 1970s, "McMillan had been designated a deputy by the sheriff of the adjoining Florida county, who in turn was authorized to make arrests in Alabama."[12]

On Monday, July 1, McMillan deputized Dr. Bill O'Bannon, a dentist at Brewton, and Charles O'Bannon, the dentist's son.

They proceeded to Florida, and McMillan hired Andrew Cunningham to locate Railroad Bill. Cunningham knew the outlaw from having previously worked with him. And he knew McMillan from having previously worked for him as a spotter. Cunningham presented a plan to the posse, which the posse accepted. On Wednesday night, July 3, the posse would stay at the house of Charles Wallace near Bluff Springs while Cunningham located Railroad Bill. Cunningham would then return and lead the men to make their arrest.[13]

Problems developed, however, when Cunningham did not return as planned. Instead, about 8:30 p.m. he sent a white man named Starks to Wallace's house with food for the posse. Starks told the men that Cunningham had located Railroad Bill in a cabin in or near the quarters of the Hughes Turpentine Company, but the outlaw was planning to leave that night for Flomaton. Cunningham directed the posse to follow Starks to make the arrest. But he warned them not to come through the village or by the railroad track, because the outlaw had been watching incoming trains since Sunday and boasting that "he would kill any man or party of men that he saw with a gun."[14]

McMillan's posse left Wallace's house with Starks under a moonlit sky. But days of rain had flooded Pritchett Mill Branch and the ford the men intended to use. Ignoring Cunningham's warning, they decided to follow the railroad track and cross the branch on the trestle. McMillan led his men by a distance of sixty to seventy feet. When he was "opposite the large oak grove that stands at the edge of the town," disaster struck. Robert Brooks, who lived nearby, heard "gun fire, and then about ten more shots."[15]

Railroad Bill had stepped out from behind a tree in the grove just after McMillan passed in front of him. Some accounts state that only one shot was fired by the outlaw, but the Brewton *Standard Gauge* states that the outlaw hailed him and immediately fired a bullet that ranged wide, causing the sheriff to turn toward the grove. A second bullet then struck him, piercing his torso near his heart and causing him to fall into a ditch, which was undoubtedly wet from recent rain.[16] Reports of what occurred next varied greatly. One stated:

> The other men then fired rapidly and as the negro came from behind the tree Dr. O'Bannon fired squarely at him bringing him down. He is confident "Railroad" is shot to pieces. But they would not go to him, lest being only wounded and in the darkness he might shoot one of them. Besides Mr. McMillan demanded their attention.
>
> They asked him if he was hurt bad. "Yes, I'm killed," he said.
>
> Brewton *Standard Gauge*, July 4, 1895

A person who conversed with Dr. O'Bannon on a train ride provided the following account:

> The posse began to move forward when suddenly from behind a tree a voice rang out, "Is that you, McMillan," and scarcely awaiting any reply a shot was fired and McMillan fell, a dead man. The posse returned the fire, as did also the negro. One of the posse, who carried a shotgun, stated that at each shot he saw the negro fall to his knees, and this created the impression that he had wounded the negro, but when the posse advanced the negro went over a bluff and in the darkness disappeared.
>
> New Orleans *Times-Democrat*, July 5, 1895

P. J. Rogers, manager of the Tennessee Coal and Iron Company at Pratt Mines, also talked with Dr. O'Bannon, and he provided the following account:

> While the posse was en route to the place and were following the directions of the white guide, they passed a rather thick place alongside of the railroad, when someone said "Hello" or "Is that you, McMillan" and almost simultaneously with the asking of the question there was the report of a gun, and the sheriff fell, mortally wounded. The posse was stunned for a minute, but recovering their self-possession in a moment they opened fire on the negro, who was recognized by some of the members of the posse. He returned the fire twice, and they could see him break his rifle and fire. He fired two shots, and then turned to make his escape, and as he ran off he was seen to fall twice, thus leading members of the posse to think that he had been hit by some of the bullets from their guns. Mr. O'Bannon stated to Mr. Rogers that it was the opinion of the posse that they had been betrayed by the negro whom they had sent to locate the negro desperado.
>
> Mobile *Daily Register*, July 5, 1895

Inconsistencies between reports of the shooting led the editor of the Pensacola *Daily News* to conduct his own inquiry. Based on his findings, he published the following to correct an earlier account in his newspaper:

> As they neared the wood-rack "Railroad" fired on Mr. Mc-Millan from behind a persimmon tree at "The Oaks." Mr. McMillan fell into a ditch by the track and after firing

a few shots the rest of the party ran and left him lying there. It was feared that, as in the case of Mr. Stewart of Bay Minette, "Railroad" would fire on whoever attempted to go to Mr. McMillan. In about half an hour Mr. T. M. Johnson, Mr. B. F. Dickson and Mr. Wallace, having found out that Sheriff McMillan was there alone, went after him and carried him to the residence of Mr. J. C. McDavid where he died about 11 o'clock.

Pensacola Daily News, July 6, 1895

Mr. Wallace was Charles Wallace, in whose house the posse was staying. T. M. Johnson was Thomas Johnson, a northerner who had been working at the Hughes Turpentine Company for about six months. B. F. Dickson was Benjamin Franklin Dickson, a foreman for the Hughes Turpentine Company. J. C. McDavid was John C. McDavid, who lived about a hundred yards from the gunfight. His house was apparently the closest refuge where the men could take the wounded sheriff.[17]

A likely scenario emerges from the reports in the press. McMillan must have realized that there was danger in crossing the branch on the trestle and therefore led his men by a distance of sixty to seventy feet. That would prove to be a safe distance for the posse, but it may have contributed to the sheriff's death. While the sheriff could not have seen Railroad Bill within the darkness created by the canopy of the grove, particularly with the outlaw behind a tree, the desperado could hear and see the officer in the moonlight approaching and passing in front of him. It is unclear if Railroad Bill was at the railroad track to assassinate the sheriff or to catch a train to Flomaton as it pulled out of Bluff Springs Station. But whatever brought him to the grove, once he saw the sheriff, his stated enemy, he did not hesitate to shoot McMillan in the back.

Railroad Bill may not have realized a posse was following McMillan as he stepped into the open and fired on the officer. Regardless, that left him between the wounded sheriff and the trailing posse, and the next gunfire was likely from the posse once they realized the situation in front of them. Dr. O'Bannon reportedly "fired squarely at [Railroad Bill] bringing him down." The outlaw "was seen to fall twice." But what Dr. O'Bannon and others in the posse may have witnessed was Railroad Bill, who was "quick as a flash and active as a kitten," jumping to the ground or to the base of a tree for safety after realizing that there were additional armed men on the railroad track.[18]

Once in the grove, Railroad Bill commanded the middle ground, and anyone advancing to assist the sheriff would have been an easy target. Dr. O'Bannon probably called to the sheriff and received the dreaded reply, "Yes, I'm killed." And with their leader down, the posse probably retreated to Wallace's house, where they had begun their quest that night. In learning of the sheriff's fate, Wallace, Johnson, and Dickson ventured to the scene in about half an hour and carried the wounded man to McDavid's house. The officer "realized his condition, said he would die, and asked those about him to pray for him."[19]

Sheriff McMillan's brother, Allen Marion McMillan (popularly known as Judge A. M. McMillan), lived at Pine Barren, eleven miles to the south. He learned of the shooting, came to his brother's bedside, and planned to take his brother home. But the officer died about an hour before midnight. Robert Brooks used diplomacy in 1931 when he explained the lack of attention given to Sheriff McMillan: "Citizens of that village were so flustered that it was some time before any effort was made to pick up the brave officer who was mortally wounded so bad that he died that night."[20]

Superintendent McKinney learned of the shooting and sent a special engine and coach to Brewton to transport Mrs. McMillan, James McMillan, doctors, deputies, and friends to Bluff Springs. By the time they arrived, there was little that could be done other than to return on the train, which was then bearing the corpse of the sheriff and his grieving widow.[21]

Later that day people were observed visiting the family residence, "some endeavoring to console the heart-broken mother and wife—others paying their last respects to the deceased friend." The funeral was held at the Brewton Methodist Church on Friday, "overflowing by sorrowing friends and sympathizers of the stricken family." The "funeral cortege was one of the longest that ever passed out of Brewton."[22]

Kate Leigh McMillan, Sheriff McMillan's widow, wore a special necklace to the funeral and during her period of mourning. She also wore it often during the remaining years of her life. It was a large black cross tipped with silver and suspended by a chain of double-conical black beads. Her descendants have made it a tradition to wear the necklace as a memorial to the fallen husband, father, and officer.[23]

10

Dragnet in the Panhandle

On Independence Day in 1895, Sheriff George Smith deputized a posse of fifteen men at Pensacola to search for Railroad Bill. Armed with repeating rifles, they boarded a special train that took them to Bluff Springs, where they were reinforced by "two dozen well-armed and indignant citizens" from Brewton. Deputy Sheriff J. W. Railey brought seven bloodhounds from the kennels of the Alabama state penitentiary to join in the search. The hounds, however, would be of little use. Heavy rain had "wiped out all scent from the ground and pursuit by the dogs had to be abandoned."[1]

At Bluff Springs, Sheriff Smith arrested Peter Robuck, Albert Williams, Henry Washington, Sallie Rankins, Mary Johnson, Lizzie Payne, and Mollie Jackson, charging each with "harboring and protecting Bill." They were transported to Pensacola and placed in jail. Andrew Cunningham was also arrested, since many believed he had "stationed 'Railroad' where he could shoot the sheriff and were in favor of shooting him." To protect Cunningham's safety, Sheriff Smith wanted to transport him to Pensacola with the other prisoners, but citizens objected. Cunningham, nevertheless, demanded and was given a hearing before a justice named Pritchett. And after reviewing the evidence, Justice Pritchett absolved Cunningham of responsibility in the sheriff's death. He was released from jail and joined a posse searching for Railroad Bill.[2]

The outlaw had fled northward after the murder and had eaten breakfast at the house of an African American at Flomaton. He then reversed direction and traveled southward, bypassing Bluff Springs, to reach Pine Barren, Florida. His decision to turn southward at Flomaton may have been influenced by the fact that a posse led by Morgan Ashe was searching trains at Bay Minette. Another posse, led by Guy Cain, was searching trains at Hurricane Bayou. Similar posses were probably posted on the two northern lines from Flomaton, one of which passed through Brewton. At Pine Barren, Railroad Bill probably stopped his southerly descent in learning that Deputy Sheriff Gordon's posse was still at Molino, another five miles to the south.[3]

The outlaw went to the home of a "respectable colored man" at Pine Barren and demanded supper. The man's description of his rude and heavily armed guest convinced authorities that it was Railroad Bill. Detective Watts and Morgan Ashe's posse were called from Alabama to assist in the search.[4]

By Friday, July 5, about forty men with bloodhounds had assembled in multiple posses searching the western panhandle for the fugitive. The only report of Railroad Bill's whereabouts, however, was an unconfirmed sighting at Sullivan's Switch near Perdido.[5] With continued failure to find the fugitive, one of the posses unleashed its wrath on individuals thought to have assisted in the outlaw's escape:

> At Flomaton on Sunday last the posse engaged in looking for Bill in that locality learned that he had been there and had found a friend in a negro man who kept an eating house, and it is stated that the posse took the negro off in the woods and administered a good lesson to him and another, and then ordered the latter to leave that section and never show his face there again. The citizens are determined that any who give Bill assistance shall fare as badly as Bill would at their hands.
>
> New Orleans *Times-Democrat*, July 10, 1895

In another incident:

> Sunday morning an old log cabin in the woods, about twenty-two miles from Flomaton, where it was rumored that the desperado was in hiding, was surrounded by the posse. No response being received to the repeated calls the house was fired into. This had the effect of bringing forth a negro man from the loft, very much frightened and exited, who, in reply to questions, denied having any knowledge of "Railroad Bill."
>
> Birmingham *Age-Herald*, July 10, 1895

After a week of fruitless searching, the bloodhounds were returned to the prison kennels, and only Sheriff Smith and a few men remained in the field.[6] A controversy was brewing by that time, based an article that originated in Montgomery and was copied in the Mobile *Daily Register*:

> A report reached here to-day from Escambia county which puts a different light on the assassination of

Sheriff McMillan, at Bluff Springs. Instead of the notorious desperado, "Railroad Bill," being charged up with the deed, the report lays it at the door of some of the sheriff's enemies down in Escambia county, of which he was the high sheriff. It is a fact that this brave man had bitter enemies in his county, some of whom were not too good to take his life's blood. The reporter's informant said this morning that he had heard from a reliable source that a conspiracy had been forged against Sheriff McMillan, and his assignation was the inevitable result of that compact: that the presence about Bluff Springs of "Railroad Bill" was a ruse to deceive the sheriff, and to entice him from home into Florida, so the crime might be better executed and made more mysterious as to the perpetrators.

This theory of the assassination finds belief in many down in Escambia. It seems very plausible when the fact is considered that no one saw "Railroad Bill" in these parts at or about that time, and the additional fact that he has made himself scarce ever since his last scrape when he killed another man who had attempted to capture him.

Mobile Daily Register, July 9, 1895

This report did not agree well with the facts. It stated that "no one saw 'Railroad Bill' in these parts at or about" the time of the sheriff's death, yet the outlaw was seen at Molino in the days leading up to the murder, at Bluff Springs on the day of the murder, and at Flomaton and Pine Barren on the day after the murder. He was identified as the shooter by the men in McMillan's posse. The article also stated that Railroad Bill "made himself scarce" after killing James Stewart, but a week after the murder he robbed the Pollard armory.[7]

To counter the accusation that someone other than Railroad Bill had killed Sheriff McMillan, the Birmingham *Age-Herald* commented that "if the late sheriff had an enemy, white or black, other than 'Railroad Bill,' no one knew it." Sheriff Dorlan declared that McMillan "had not made himself obnoxious to the people of Escambia county, but on the other hand that he had enforced the law firmly but kindly, and that there was nothing of the bully or bravado about the dead sheriff." He added that during the Mount Vernon manhunt, McMillan "felt that his life was in danger." McMillan also said that "'Railroad Bill' would not hesitate to shoot either one of them in the dark if they should happen to pass him."[8]

Rewards for Railroad Bill included $350 by the L&N Railroad, $150 by the governor of Alabama, $300 by the citizens of Brewton, $250 by Escambia County, and $200 by the governor of Florida: a total of $1,250 offered for capturing or killing the notorious desperado.[9]

Superintendent McKinney believed that the State of Alabama should offer a larger reward after losing one of its law-enforcement officers. He and L&N attorney J. M. Faulkner met with Governor Oates to encourage him to raise the state's offering, but the governor refused, citing depleted funds in the state treasury.[10]

About a week after the sheriff's murder, a freight-train crew saw Railroad Bill at Atmore just as their train was pulling away from Williams Station.[11] Detective Watts also saw the desperado on that occasion:

It is supposed that [Railroad Bill] boarded a freight train from Flomaton, alighting a few yards beyond the station house at Williams. He passed along the track immediately in front of the station in which were Watts and a negro confidant. The detective arose quickly and went to the door, from which he had a good view of the passing negro, who was positively identified as "Railroad Bill."

A gentleman who spent the night at Bay Minette was unable to say why an encounter did not take place between the detective and the desperado but supposed it was because Watts was armed at the time only with his revolver.

A posse composed of six or eight men and dogs armed with guns and revolvers was immediately organized and started in pursuit of the negro.

Brewton *Standard Gauge*, July 18, 1985

The next day, Railroad Bill was seen about two miles from Daphne. He made his presence known by boldly stepping from the shadows beside Fish River Road to engage W. C. Turner, a local merchant, in conversation:

Mr. Turner was driving and the negro raised from behind a log and hailed him. Mr. Turner stopped and the negro came up and put one foot on the hub of the front wheel, and his hand on the seat, and talked to Mr. Turner about half an hour. He said that he was "Railroad," and on being asked if he was going to Daphne, he replied: "No, I am close enough."

Mr. Turner asked him where he came from and he said that this morning at daylight he was near Bay Minette. Mr. Turner then asked him where he was going, and he replied: "I am going about my business, when I get ready. Why?"

Mr. Turner replied: "Nothing."

Then Railroad asked: "Do you want me?"

Mr. Turner replied: "No."

Mr. Turner describes him as a yellow negro, about thirty-five years old, wearing a "crusher" hat, a dark colored "jumper" jacket and dark cotton trousers, stripped; also a good pair of lace shoes with heavy soles.

Mr. Turner left the negro where he found him and continued on the road leading away from Daphne. In coming back about an hour later, he saw another negro about half a mile from where he saw Railroad, whom he described as yellow, about twenty years old, and weighing about 150 pounds. This last negro said that he was from Bay Minette and was going to Kapahn's store (Baldwin's store) on Fish river. This last negro is thought to be a confederate of Railroad, or a spy, and leads to the belief that Railroad is going to Baldwin's store to get supplies or whisky.

Railroad carries a large canteen, and he was asked by Mr. Turner what he did with it, and replied that he kept water in it when he could not get whisky.

Brewton Pine Belt News, July 13, 1895

Following the death of Sheriff McMillan, his brother, Judge A. M. McMillan, actively joined in the search to capture or kill Railroad Bill. He questioned Turner's account and said, "I immediately sent a man down into Baldwin county to see Turner. The first thing he said upon seeing me was: 'The man Turner saw was undoubtedly Railroad Bill.'"[12]

Some suspected that Railroad Bill would go from Daphne to Blakeley, where he reportedly had a "sweetheart." The village was located on the bank of the Blakely River, about halfway to Hurricane Bayou. But no report indicated that he went to Blakely.[13]

Meanwhile, back in Escambia County, Alabama, the office of sheriff was still vacant. Governor Oates did not appoint a successor before leaving the state three days after the murder to conduct business in Washington, D.C. James McMillan was filling the void, serving as chief deputy and directing other deputies as he had done when he was sheriff between 1886 and 1892. Citizens petitioned the governor on July 10 to appoint James as sheriff. But it would be another five days before the governor responded in a telegram making the appointment.[14] By that time a newspaper editor in Covington County, indignant over the failure of officers to capture Railroad Bill, was indirectly calling for activation of the state militia:

> The state of Alabama has a large number of soldiers and pays them for their services. They are nice looking soft skinned fellows with blue suits, brass buttons, caps and gun. They are a showy crowd and when they go into encampment they break all the girls' hearts and run all the little negro boys out of town. One little negro desperado comes into the state, kills a few of our best citizens and goes on defying the law and the soldier boys stay close for fear they will get their feet damp, take cold, and be unfit for service.
>
> Covington *Times*, July 12, 1895

Activation of the militia was not needed. A small army of bounty hunters was mustering in southern Alabama, hoping to collect all or part of the reward money. "From now on," the Pensacola *Daily News* commented, "the trail promises to be exceedingly warm. The $1,250 reward will attract the slickest 'sleuthhounds' in the country." Two of the sleuthhounds were Pinkerton detectives from Chicago who were seen passing through Montgomery on July 11 to join an estimated fifty men in the search. Mr. Peeples of Wetumpka also passed through with "a pack of fine hounds" from the kennels of the state penitentiary.[15]

It would seem that Railroad Bill deliberately made his presence known at Daphne before leaving for the Mississippi Gulf Coast to avoid law officers, railroad detectives, and bounty hunters scouring southern Alabama and western Florida. On Monday, July 15, he was seen at Biloxi "in company with a woman." Later, and in succession, he was reported at Moss Point, Pass Christian, and Mississippi City. Captain Ben Duckworth and a posse sought to capture the notorious fugitive, and on one occasion "struck a cabin in the woods where Bill's cot was yet warm, and was told he had been there."[16]

A posse of railroad detectives responded from Alabama, arriving by train at West End Station near Pass Christian on July 25. Deputy Postal Inspector Luke Jones said the men carried rifles and shotguns and acted as if "they had received a 'straight tip' on the whereabouts of the negro and were almost sure of capturing the red-handed assassin." Passengers on the train told Jones that Railroad Bill had been hiding with friends near Pass Christian for several days. But he had an argument, and the friends reported his whereabouts to authorities.[17] The outlaw's hiding place was thought to be in Wolf River swamp north of Pass Christian:

> There is a portion of Harrison county in the western part where Wolf river flows, which is inhabited mainly by negroes, whose huts are far apart. The roads and highways

of this section are rather crooked and intricate, and while the unacquainted traveler would travel miles from point to point, the average citizen can take a short cut through the swamp and brakes, with which the section abounds. The society reports are not kept up in this section, consequently the public don't know everything that is going on, neither is there a record of births, deaths and marriages kept, hence a stranger might die in these wilds and his family would never know what disposition was made of his remains, or what the verdict of the coroner's jury might be. There are, however, visitors to these wilds occasionally, and it is a favorite resort of criminals who desire to keep from the public gaze for a while, and it is a well known resort of the irrepressible Railroad Bill, who is so badly wanted, and there is every reason to believe that that individual was there only a few days before he made his late reappearance over in Alabama.

New Orleans *Daily Picayune*, August 10, 1895

Railroad Bill returned to Baldwin County, taking refuge in a secure hideout in Honeycut Creek swamp, three miles north of Hurricane Bayou:

A gentleman from Baldwin county stated to the correspondent of The Times-Democrat to-day that he was assured that "Railroad Bill" was still in the neighborhood of Hurricane Bayou. He represented that Bill was at home in this section, and supplied with every necessity and luxuries in many instances, by his colored admirers, with whose assistance, and his own knowledge of the woodcraft, he was entirely able to outwit his pursuers, and even to lay a trap for them at any time he desired. To quote the gentleman, "Bill is now in Honeycut Creek swamp, waiting for the excitement to die out, when he will again venture forth." The man said he "has fifteen miles to play in, and to one of his nature it is an easy matter to escape detectives, unless the party be supplied with a good dog to trail him." He has not abated a jot of his former boldness and some days ago he procured a negro to go to a store and purchase a package of cheroots for him.

New Orleans Times-Democrat, July 26, 1895

The Honeycut Creek hideout was strategically located and probably once used by Railroad Bill's freight-car gang. To the west were rivers, bays, and bayous forming the Mobile-Tensaw River delta, the nation's second-largest river delta.

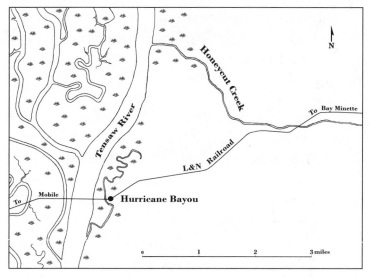

Honeycut Creek swamp, where Railroad Bill maintained a hideout.

Bloodhounds would have been of little use in tracking a man escaping by boat. To the east were bottomlands that extended several miles toward Bay Minette. To the north and south were marshlands forming the eastern periphery of the delta. A person who knew the lay of the land could move about, but a stranger would fumble to find his way.

If the Honeycut Creek hideout was used by Railroad Bill's gang, they could have descended on the railroad station at Hurricane Bayou at night, a person could have been placed in a freight car while the train was stopped at the station or water tank, and once the train was under way, merchandise could have been thrown out until the train slowed on a steep grade two miles west of Bay Minette. The person could then have jumped out to return to his comrades gathering merchandise beside the track. Since the headwaters of Honeycut Creek passed below the track near the grade, the men could follow it, even on a dark night, to return to their hideout near the mouth of the creek. By wading the creek, the men would leave little scent for bloodhounds to follow. Authorities discovered the hideout by a tip:

Yesterday afternoon a little negro boy came running up to the posse and reported that Railroad and an armed force were camped near the mouth of one of the rivers in the vicinity of Bay Minette. They had a cabin well stocked with provisions, and every man was heavily armed, and if they were disturbed they intend to make a fight.

Some of the posse descended the river in boats, while others made a circuit for the purpose of surprising the gang from the rear.

Pensacola *Daily News*, July 26, 1895

The attack on the Honeycut Creek hideout failed to capture Railroad Bill. It became another in a long list of failures by law officers. It also preceded Railroad Bill's most celebrated escape, an exasperating weeklong episode that became known as the Castleberry chase.

11

The Castleberry Chase

Railroad Bill was reported near Hammac, Alabama, on Monday, July 29, 1895, about four days after lawmen raided his Honeycut Creek hideout. He killed a bird that morning and had it cooked by someone at a nearby house. He then began an eleven-mile walk eastward toward Brewton. It marked the beginning of the Castleberry chase.[1]

On the road the desperado happened upon another African American and commanded, "If you have got any money, let's have it." The man yielded fifty cents. Near Brewton, Railroad Bill crossed Burnt Corn Creek at Holland Bridge. Henry Terry's daughter saw him while she was gathering peaches in an orchard. He passed over farmland owned by the Robbins, Padgett, and Foshee families. On the Foshee farm he talked at length with an African American named Samson Sherrill. Fearing reprisal, Sherrill "failed to give the alarm until late in the afternoon." Railroad Bill spent the night in a house near the canning factory on the outskirts of town.[2]

A posse of four men led by T. J. Kenrick had followed Railroad Bill after finding his trail early in the day near the house where the bird had been cooked. By 5:00 p.m. they were within a couple of miles of Brewton and decided to stop for the night.[3]

Citizens were alarmed Tuesday morning to discover that the desperado had practically spent the night in town. "It is thought," the Brewton *Standard Gauge* commented, "that it is the daredevil in him that caused him to venture so near Brewton. He says there are three more men here he wants to kill."[4]

On Tuesday morning, reinforcements from Brewton, Kirkland, and Evergreen joined the posse. Bloodhounds were also brought down from kennels of the state penitentiary near Speigner Station on the L&N Railroad northwest of Wetumpka.[5]

The hounds located Railroad Bill's scent four miles north of Brewton in J. M. Padgett's field near Downing's Tank. The desperado had stopped there to eat ground peas and watermelon that morning before continuing northward. The hounds "opened up lively" from the field, and when the posse crossed the L&N track from Brewton to Montgomery, the dogs' behavior indicated to Mr. Massengale, their handler, that the fugitive was only about twenty minutes ahead of them. They continued to follow the outlaw until they reached Murder Creek where the trail ended. Railroad Bill had entered the flow and waded upstream. The posse crossed the creek, and the hounds found where he had emerged. The dogs' disposition then told Massengale that he was nearby in the thick terrain. The hounds were unleashed.[6]

Danger lurked for men who followed an armed fugitive into thick undergrowth. At any time the fleeing man could attack from a position of advantage. It was customary, therefore, to unleash the hounds. The baying of the dogs would betray the position of the fugitive, regardless of whether he was running, hiding, climbing a tree, or setting a trap.

Authorities in every state were using bloodhounds to track convicts. A variety of breeds were being employed. Some were mongrels, beagles, or foxhounds that tracked well and demonstrated good perseverance, yet they "would not fight unless in such large numbers that they gained courage from this fact." More aggressive breeds had been used during war, but they were considered too vicious for use with convicts. One such breed was the Cuban bloodhound, a cross between a mastiff and a bulldog. It was "a most ferocious and dangerous beast" that would "pull down a man and throttle and tear him." Authorities in Alabama were using bloodhounds "of English strain and breeding, a cross between the famous Redbone hound and the great beagle." They were considered aggressive, but they would generally not attack unless the fugitive was running or attempting to attack them. The breed had distinguished itself in trailing Rube Burrow, and offspring had been sold for use by authorities as far away as Indiana.[7]

The hounds overtook Railroad Bill about three-quarters of a mile from Murder Creek. He fired twice, causing the dogs to return to the posse and refuse to trail. Without the hounds as forward pickets, the posse stalled. Railroad Bill continued eastward toward Brooklyn and Andalusia, Alabama, putting distance between himself and his pursuers.[8]

Later, the posse again found Railroad Bill's trail. He was heading for a big swamp.[9] The men planned to surround and surprise him at the swamp, but as Sheriff McMillan explained later, they failed:

We would have caught the scoundrel the other day when we had him partly hemmed in a swamp—it was the time he killed that dog and shot a hole through Mr. Tom [Charles] Dyer's hat, but a fool detective, or alleged detective, saw a wild turkey, shot at it several times, and this disgusted my men. I didn't blame them of course. "Bill" was warned and got away.

Montgomery Daily Advertiser, August 6, 1895

The desperado passed through the swamp and again distanced himself from the posse. His trail was located once again late in the afternoon, and the dogs followed it to a little church about two and a half miles east of Castleberry. It was the end of the day, and the posse made camp for the night.[10] The next morning the trail was difficult to find and most of the day was spent looking for it. Conecuh County sheriff I. R. Irwin explained:

We lost all trace of "Railroad Bill" this morning, but struck his trail again this evening and tracked him to a house near Castleberry. He was seen about 11 o'clock a.m. by two reliable white boys and a negro woman, all of them giving accurate descriptions of "Railroad." He was then about two miles south of Castleberry on the east side of Murder Creek in the swamps. From that point we trailed him about one and a half miles north of Castleberry on the east side of Murder Creek to a woman's house, who, it was understood, he was going to see. The house was deserted, but about sundown a party saw him with this woman near Castleberry.

Montgomery Daily Advertiser, August 1, 1895

Men were posted near the house that night, and the Castleberry depot was "turned into a guard house." African Americans passing through the area were detained at the depot and not "permitted to go about for fear they might sneak some information to 'Railroad.'"[11]

The *Daily Advertiser* warned that "it will be little less than a beneficent miracle if some of the large posse do not die at the hands of this man who has so many murders and robberies charged to his account."[12] But the next morning there was no bloodshed:

> "Railroad" was "flushed" out of a negro's cabin by two of the posse who came up within fifty yards of him. "Railroad" is said to have leveled his rifle at the men, and, backing off, ordered that the one who raised his arm would get killed. "Railroad" commanded the men to halt where they were while he continued to walk backwards and finally got entirely away without either of the huntsmen taking a shot at him.
>
> Montgomery *Daily Advertiser*, August 2, 1895

Superintendent McKinney, "whose determination to bag 'Railroad' is as strong as ever," had joined the posse Thursday morning. They found Railroad Bill's trail, which led from the house where he had spent the night, and followed it until they were close enough to unleash the hounds. This time the outlaw killed the lead dog, "worth over a hundred dollars," and the remaining hounds once more refused to trail.[13] F. E. Brawner, a merchant visiting relatives in Castleberry, sent a note back to Pensacola:

> They are close after Railroad Bill here to-day. There are about 15 mounted men, 30 on foot and 7 bloodhounds. Three of the dogs closed in on him an hour ago, others being held in reserve. Railroad Bill shot at them three

times. It is not known how many were killed, as only one has been brought in yet. His capture is expected at any minute as his pursuers are determined men.

Pensacola *Daily News*, August 2, 1895

Judge McMillan had been with the posse, but that morning he had taken a train from Castleberry to Mobile to attend a business engagement. Superintendent McKinney sent a telegram requesting that he "come back at once and get the men to go in the swamp after [Railroad Bill]."[14]

Considering the wording in McKinney's telegram and the fact that McMillan was "head of the McMillan mill Company, which gave employment to hundreds of people," one might conclude that members of the posse were being paid by McMillan. Accordingly, when McMillan reached Mobile, he remained at the station for the next train back to Castleberry. While he waited, he told a reporter that twenty to twenty-five men were in the posse and that he thought they would capture or kill Railroad Bill before he could return.[15]

McKinney sent another telegram to a Mr. Vass, one of his clerks at Union Station:

> Can you see the Governor and get him to get us six or more dogs. Our men struck "Railroad's" trail one mile back of Castleberry and run it thirty minutes, when he killed one of the dogs, shooting it twice. This was about 9:30 this morning. He is within one mile of here.
>
> Montgomery *Daily Advertiser*, August 2, 1895

Governor Oates was in Florence, Alabama, but had left a secretary named Varden at Union Station to telegraph information to him. It is unclear if Varden relayed McKinney's request, but additional bloodhounds were not forthcoming from the state. Colonel R. H. Dawson, the state superintendent of convicts, had authority over the prison's kennel and refused, saying that "the dogs had already done all they could, which was to trail and 'tree' the negro; that they couldn't go into a swamp or a house and arrest 'Railroad' and bring him out."[16]

McKinney's request would instead be fulfilled by officials with Pratt Mines near Birmingham. The mines used large numbers of state-leased convicts and kept a kennel of bloodhounds, of which six were placed on a train scheduled to arrive at Castleberry that night.[17]

Bloodhounds, however, would often prove to be of limited value in trailing Railroad Bill. Some stated reasons included rain that washed away the outlaw's scent, the heat of summer that interfered with the dogs' ability to follow a scent, multiple tracks that confused the trail, and the outlaw's deadly aim. There was also the possibility that "the reason Railroad Bill has been so successful in keeping the dogs off his scent is by applying turpentine to the sole of his shoes." In a forest of pine, the derivative of pine may have worked.[18]

In the afternoon, Judge McMillan returned to the posse near Castleberry, and his brother Sheriff James McMillan arrived about 4:00 p.m. with fifteen to twenty deputies from Brewton. The men reentered the swamp in the area where the dog had been killed. They scattered in all directions looking for the fugitive until shots rang out in a thicket. Charles Dyer of Flomaton had walked up on Railroad Bill, who was hidden behind two crossed logs. One bullet from the outlaw perforated Dyer's hat brim. Although Dyer could not see his adversary, he returned fire eight times.[19]

The posse's dread had been realized. Without hounds leading the way, each man was a potential target. The dogs were brought to where Dyer had exchanged gunshots with the fugitive, but "there being so many other tracks they could do nothing, and the desperado escaped." It was near the end of a long day, and the search was halted with "at least 100 men here 'loaded for bear,' and ready for to-morrow." Superintendent McKinney sent a telegram to Trainmaster Frank Gault: "Whatever you do, have all trains run through Castleberry south at a fast gait. He is fixing to take a train if possible." Judge McMillan sent a telegram to his son Frank in Pensacola: "We will have six good dogs on No. 3 tonight and have a good chance for to-morrow."[20]

R. L. Rouse, a Pinkerton agent from North Carolina, claimed to have encountered Railroad Bill on the previous Thursday, which would have been about the time the posse raided the Honeycut Creek hideout. Rouse said he walked up on the outlaw, who was sitting on a log in a cluster of bushes.[21] The desperado commanded him to stop:

> I reckon you are after me, said [Railroad Bill], dropping a bird, which he had been cleaning, into his pocket. Anybody with you, he asked. I told him no and in turn asked him where he was going. None of your d——n business, was his reply. I'm a d——n good mind to stop you from following me, but I guess you want to get a nip at that reward. You can't do it though, and I aint afraid of the whole push of you. Railroad backed off, keeping me covered.
>
> Montgomery *Daily Advertiser*, August 6, 1895

About midnight the Pratt bloodhounds arrived at Evergreen Station on a train to Castleberry. There had been a report, which turned out to be false, of Railroad Bill near the station, so the dogs were taken off the train and placed into service. Their effort, of course, was futile. The Montgomery *Daily Advertiser* commented, "'His Foxy Highness' is making it exceedingly interesting for the posse. . . . But withal, it does seem that a hundred men with dogs and guns, should trap the scoundrel."[22]

The next day, Friday, August 2, marked the end of the chase for Railroad Bill near Castleberry. The outlaw was reportedly seen in the afternoon about three miles south of town. But rain all day prevented the dogs from following his trail. Three of the four hounds from the state prison kennels were returned, and many of the men who had participated in the hunt went home exhausted.[23] One of the men who returned to Montgomery addressed the public's growing cynicism of the Castleberry chase:

> You people up here have not the least idea of the true state of affairs in and around that cussed swamp. To begin with the swamp is rendered almost impenetrable by a dense growth of thick, low underbrush, besides being filled with marshes, bogs, etc. It would be well nigh impossible to catch a negro though he were in plain view if he had any ways the start of you, and just think how it is with this Slater negro. He is well armed, desperate, perfectly familiar with the swamp, and instead of going blundering around through bogs, briers, and bad woods all he has to do is to lay perfectly still and be hunted.
>
> Mobile *Daily Register*, August 4, 1895

Reports of Railroad Bill did not end with the Castleberry chase. According to Sheriff McMillan, he was seen on Saturday at 5:00 p.m. near Brewton:

> Three youths, one of whom is the son of Postmaster Rankin, of Brewton, were wandering about in the woods near the canning factory for some purpose, when they met a negro. The young men, being familiar with "Railroad's" description, at once thought it was him. He asked them what they were doing out there, and they evidently gave him a satisfactory reply. He then questioned them about his pursuers and told them point blank: "I am Railroad Bill."
>
> Now this isn't the first time he has bragged about himself in this manner, and it is a natural result of his successful career of crime and dodging of officers. I think that he believes himself invincible.
>
> Montgomery *Daily Advertiser*, August 6, 1895

The announcement of Railroad Bill's return to Brewton caused understandable excitement:

> Every train brought men form each direction, and citizens reported for duty. A freight engine turned around at Castleberry when the news reached there and brought six fine hounds with several detectives who have been chasing the dare-devil for several days. In the meantime, and before the best dogs arrived, a local hound had taken the negro's back trail and continued on it some time, followed by a body of horsemen and others on foot, who searched empty houses and looked in every nook and

corner for the negro, but to no avail. At night the hunt was abandoned until the morrow. The swamp near town is a splendid hiding place for criminals, though not as dense as Castleberry Thursday. It is supposed that Bill is making his way back to his old haunts in Baldwin County.

Montgomery Daily Advertiser, August 4, 1895

The posse's failure to hem in the outlaw served to reinforce the belief of many authorities that a small, handpicked posse led by a professional detective might have a better chance for success:

There are entirely too many men after him to ever effect his capture. A dozen men and the bloodhounds now here would soon run to earth the daring rascal, if Tom, Dick and Harry and nearly everybody else did not have a gun, rifle or musket on their shoulders, some wishing that they never would see Bill alive. Such determined men as Jackson, Barnes, Gordon, Tremer, Tom Dower and many others seem to think that his capture is only a matter of a few days. If a trail can be struck to-morrow these men say they will capture their game before night. Bill has every advantage, even over a hundred pursuers, for he lies in a dense clump of bushes, and can see and hear a man coming long before he gets to him. He is a cunning culprit, and on every occasion has completely outwitted and bewildered those searching for him.

Pensacola Daily News, August 5, 1895

Two Montgomery reporters traveled to Brewton on Sunday, August 4, to cover the aftermath of the Castleberry chase. After registering at the Ahren House Hotel, they took chairs on the veranda to watch the activities of people on one of the main streets in town:

> The passing throng and general scene suggested a frontier town on the eve of an expected attack by Indians. Mingled among the good folks on their way to church, squads of men with Winchesters and braces of revolvers passed along, sometimes stopping to chat with horsemen—scouts they seemed—carrying guns across the pommels of their saddles.
>
> Montgomery *Daily Advertiser*, August 6, 1895

As the reporters watched, news of another sighting of the desperado reached the streets. While traveling to Kirkland, Mrs. J. E. McGowan observed an armed suspect near the road who fit Railroad Bill's description. Upon arrival, she sent her son back to Brewton to sound the alarm.[24] A posse was assembled, and the reporters followed as observers:

> A glimpse of the country which is splotched at close intervals with swamps made clear the reason why "Railroad" has had such an easy time evading his pursuers, and then, when one is in the steps of a man who is absolutely desperate, a dead shot, and liable to assassinate one from ambush at any time, one is not so eager to pursue.
>
> Montgomery *Daily Advertiser*, August 6, 1895

The posse found no evidence of Railroad Bill. Repeated failures to bring the desperado to justice prompted the Brewton *Pine Belt News* to write, "Wm. is a slick duck—entirely too much for all who have been hunting(!) him around the depots here and at Castleberry."[25]

Authorities had concluded that a small posse of dedicated

men led by a proven officer would have a better chance of capturing the outlaw than the dozens of men who had been hunting the fugitive near Castleberry. Detective D. W. Barnes of Birmingham, who had extensive experience in apprehending criminals, was appointed to lead a handpicked posse. Barnes began by creating a map of reported sightings of Railroad Bill. After analyzing the map, he concluded that most of the reports were unreliable, merely "fabrications by fellows who are trying to keep up the excitement and hold their summer job, pulling the railroad for passes and expenses."[26] William Stallworth, one of Barnes's handpicked men in the posse, shared that view:

> Among the very numerous detectives hunting Railroad is a man by the name of Hendrix. He claims to be from Texas and has a negro with him who he says helps him with all of his detective cases. Time after time I have asked him to let me talk to this negro, but he always puts me off with some trivial excuse. The negro has never been seen by a single person in or around Brewton. Hendrix gave me as references the names of several chiefs of police in some Texas towns, but when I wired them they invariably answered by saying that they had never seen or heard of Hendrix or the negro.
>
> Friday night I asked for the negro again, and Hendrix said he would send him to my room. In about an hour he—Hendrix—came up and said the negro had not come up yet. Now, if this is not fishy, what is it? My idea is, that the negro who Hendrix speaks of is one of the redoubtable triplet Railroad Bill's himself, and that he and Hendrix are working somebody down to a fine point.
>
> Montgomery *Daily Advertiser*, August 7, 1895

When asked what motive Hendrix could have for staging fake reports, Stallworth replied, "To keep up the excitement and draw pay from the L. and N."[27]

With Detective Barnes shouldering primary responsibility for capturing Railroad Bill, some of the burden was removed from Sheriff McMillan. Yet he was finding his new job particularly challenging. His brother had spent most of the last month of his life in the field searching for the outlaw. The new sheriff now confronted a backlog of warrants and duties. Meanwhile, he was receiving criticism from people who viewed the Castleberry chase as "a waste of time."[28] And he was stressed regarding the feelings of his wife and mother:

> Mr. McMillan's mother is a venerable lady 76 years old, and since her loss of the son, she had begged and implored the present sheriff not to follow "Bill" lest he too, might be killed. The mother's entreaties have been no less ardent than those of the wife, this anxiety, the fearful mental pain and apprehension, has caused the illness of both ladies.
>
> For a time Sheriff McMillan heeded their pleadings and this brought on more criticism. "He should go out after Bill—is he afraid?" Some would say. Now these remarks reached the ears of the Sheriff who is undoubtedly a brave man, and he was determined to lead the chase.
>
> Montgomery *Daily Advertiser*, August 6, 1895

Railroad Bill was being reported in areas other than Brewton. Near Monroeville, forty miles northwest of Brewton, Charles Busey's children came home on August 7 and told their father that they had walked up on a man in the woods. They said the man had a rifle and was relaxing beneath a large tree, but when he saw them he jumped to his feet and ran, leaving an article of clothing. A posse searched but could not find the suspect.[29]

On August 9 in Birmingham, two hundred miles north of Monroeville, a report of Railroad Bill was made. Sheriff George Morrow and a posse of deputies, policemen, and citizens responded to the "rumor" that Railroad Bill was in the city. "Several houses were searched and the hunt prosecuted with diligence," but the outlaw "with a big price on his head" could not be found.[30]

Detective Watts also reported that he "was positive he had seen the outlaw near Castleberry Friday morning [August 9]," but he "had no force of men with which to effect his capture."[31] There was also a report on August 9 of Railroad Bill being on the Mississippi Gulf Coast. John C. Craig, Captain Ben Duckworth's deputy, was driving a hack near De Buys Station when

> He was suddenly confronted by a tall negro with a bright Winchester rifle slung over his shoulder, who looked at him in a dare devil and suspicious manner. Craig had a description of Railroad Bill in his pocket and has been on the lay for him. His first impulse was to stop, but a second glance at the face and aspect of the man induced him to drive on, which he did, and at once proceeded to inform Captain Duckworth of his meeting the negro. The negro was heading towards Biloxi and was about two miles from Mississippi City.
>
> New Orleans *Daily Picayune*, August 10, 1895

Detective Barnes, four heavily armed men, and bloodhounds from Barnes's kennel in Jamison, Alabama, arrived at Mississippi City by train. They were reinforced by Captain Duckworth and Deputies J. C. Craig and Frank Duckworth, and the posse followed the beach road to Biloxi and then entered the woods. "It is supposed," the New Orleans *Daily Picayune* wrote, "that the fugitive is making his way to his old haunts about Wolf river." But Railroad Bill could not be found.[32]

On August 13, 1895, the *Daily Picayune* reported that Mobile County sheriff Phelan Dorlan had received a letter from an officer in Houston who had a suspect in jail who fit Railroad Bill's description. It was not Railroad Bill, just another dubious report. In an interview at the Battle House Hotel in Mobile, Judge A. M. McMillan was asked about the flurry of Railroad Bill sightings. "I receive numbers of them every day," McMillan said, "and he is invariably located forty or fifty miles apart. I have gotten so that I pay little attention to them."[33]

12

Unintended Victims

The large reward offered for Railroad Bill dead or alive produced unintended consequences. The first involved an African American named Bill Vaughn, who voluntarily surrendered at the Pensacola police station on July 13, 1895, for shooting Abe Walton. Vaughn told the officers that Walton came to his farmhouse the previous afternoon and asked for food and a place to sleep. Vaughn agreed and asked his wife to provide supper and a pallet on the floor. Walton carried a large pistol and $150 which he said he had won gambling with a deputy sheriff. He also said that he was going to Pensacola to find Andrew Cunningham, the detective who had assisted Sheriff McMillan when the sheriff was killed by Railroad Bill.[1]

The next morning Walton offered Vaughn a horse that he had secured nearby. The men started to see the horse and hadn't gone far before Walton stopped and said that he had to go back to retrieve a Winchester and a box of cartridges that he had left behind a log. Walton's behavior, pistol, Winchester, money, and mention of Cunningham made Vaughn believe that he was Railroad Bill. The farmer hurried home and told his wife that their visitor had killed Sheriff McMillan.[2]

Vaughn loaded a musket with buckshot and went to the house of a neighbor, a German named Andrew, and from the gate he called for Andrew. But to his surprise, Walton opened the door. As Walton turned to say something to Andrew, Vaughn jumped the fence, sneaked up to the house, and shouted: "Andrew, that is the man who killed the sheriff. There is $500 reward for him. Tie him! Tie him!! I say."[3]

Walton ran into the yard, turning his pistol toward Vaughn. But seeing that he was covered by Vaughn's musket, he turned and ran with Vaughn shouting for him to stop. Vaughn fired, striking Walton in the back.[4]

The wounded man was taken in critical condition to the city infirmary and attended by city physician Dr. H. L. Simpson, assisted by Dr. Pierpoint. Vaughn then went to the police station to tell his story. Justice Boykin Jones and Andrew Cunningham went to the infirmary, and Cunningham verified that the wounded man was not Railroad Bill.[5]

Walton's story contradicted Vaughn's. Walton said he did not have a pistol or a rifle. He had been working in a logging camp near Repton before coming to Pensacola, and Vaughn knew that he was not Railroad Bill. But, Walton claimed, in a dispute over payment for room and board, Vaughn shot him and passed him off as the desperado.[6]

In subsequent interviews, Vaughn made conflicting statements, which made it difficult for authorities to discern the truth. Thus, on July 17 a summons was served on the much-improved Walton, who was still in the infirmary. It required him to appear before the county solicitor the next week. But at 5:00 a.m. the next day, Walton secretly left the hospital and afterward was not seen about the city. His exit convinced authorities "that he was a fugitive from some point."[7]

Another case of mistaken identity occurred in August 1895 near Chipley, Georgia. The victim was not as fortunate as Walton, and his body was transported to Montgomery for identification as Railroad Bill. It was accompanied by O. D. Hardy, the marshal of Chipley, and John S. Garner, the father of the man who killed the suspect. Marshal Hardy explained that Sheriff J. H. Henderson of Troup County, Georgia, had offered a reward for two fugitives. Willis Garner and John A. Garner thought they had located the fugitives at a house about a mile and a half from Chipley. The Garners approached the suspects on the back porch and commanded them to hold up their hands. Both obeyed. Then one of the men took several steps, pulled out a revolver, and fired, striking Willis Garner in the stomach. Willis fell, still holding his Marlin rifle in his hands. John grabbed the shooter by the wrist, and the two men began to tussle. Willis rose on his elbows and fired, striking the suspect in the left side near the stomach. The bullet passed through the individual's body and exited near the back of the neck.[8]

When the first shot was fired, the other suspect started to flee. But being beckoned by his comrade, he returned, and before making his escape he fired "promiscuously" without hitting anyone. He was identified as "Marshall Williams, a negro gambler who had been loafing around Chipley."[9]

Marshal Hardy was called to the house and found Willis with a painful wound that was not life threatening. The suspect was on the floor where he had fallen, mortally wounded. In his pockets the marshal found several packs of cards, a ticket to Pensacola, and a reward circular for Railroad Bill. When asked why he had Railroad Bill's description in his pocket, the victim "became confused asking what description and trying to get out of having it." The wounded man lived another eight hours, during which the marshal repeatedly asked if he was Railroad Bill. The only reply given was, "Maybe I am, and maybe I ain't."[10]

Man Culpepper owned the house. He said he knew nothing about either suspect. They had simply asked for a place to sleep. He was away when the shooting started but heard the shots and ran back to the house. The suspect wounded on the floor handed him a purse with six dollars in it and said, "Send this to my wife, Ida Bell Williams, at 306 Texas Street, Mobile, Ala." Later, Culpepper's wife wrote to Williams, informing her that her husband had been killed. Mrs. Culpepper added: "The colored people here desire to know if there was anything like a crime against him. Please answer at once, so that we can understand the matter."[11]

Marshal Hardy and the Garners, believing the victim was Railroad Bill, had the body transported to Montgomery for official identification. After it arrived by train and was placed on the landing dock at Union Station, the news spread about the city, and a crowd gathered, "indulging in the most remarkable speculation among themselves." The face was swollen, making the corpse difficult to recognize, yet it was similar to Railroad Bill's published description. The complexion was a dark copper color, the cheekbones were prominent, and it had a scar that passed from below the left eye to the tip of the ear. It was dressed in a worn hickory shirt, light trousers, and a slouch hat. The shoes were one size different from those reported in the description. But the Montgomery *Daily Advertiser* commented that it was not likely that "one pair of shoes will last two or three months after being worn through swamps and other bad country."[12]

Edward Mershon, the train engineer who had been held hostage by Railroad Bill in the Hurricane Bayou gunfight, viewed the body. A trainman named Rylander, who had exchanged gunshots with the outlaw, also viewed the body. They agreed with others that it was not the notorious desperado. On August 17 the L&N had the body interred in an unmarked grave in Potter's Field at Montgomery. The corpse was eventually identified as that of William Thomas, one of three brothers whom Captain Hughes had brought to Alabama along with Railroad Bill.[13]

Ida Bell Williams said that William Thomas had lived with her in Mobile until about three weeks before his death. He "was a hard-working, well behaved" man, she said, and did not know Railroad Bill. Nevertheless, after they had a fight, he left to avoid an arrest. But authorities believed that he left to avoid a more serious charge than wife beating. He was wanted for killing a deputy sheriff in Henry County, Alabama, on May 3, 1895, and an $800 reward was offered for his capture.[14]

There was much speculation regarding the identity and crimes of William Thomas and two of his brothers, George and Gus Thomas.[15] The following report seems to satisfy most questions regarding William and George:

The following telegram was received from Flomaton, proving several things conclusively. The first is that the negro killed by Mr. Garner in Chipley was a bigger fish than was thought—the wife-beating story was more a bluff than anything else—another is that Garner will get either $800 [for killing William Thomas] or $500 reward [for killing George Thomas], for there is no doubt that the dead negro was one of the two described in the telegram, though the description of George answers his appearance best. The fact remains that the Thomas negroes were desperate characters, and a great deal better dead than alive. Another strong point in favor of the theory of the negro being a pal of Railroad's is that he came from Railroad's old haunts, worked in a turpentine still and is just as desperate as Railroad Bill could possibly be.

Pensacola Daily News, August 19, 1895

The Thomas brothers had been brought to Baldwin County with Railroad Bill by Captain Hughes as laborers to work in his turpentine camp. In 1890, Gus Thomas dueled with conductor Breck McCurdy on an L&N train near Mobile. Gus died on the train; McCurdy died later of wounds received. In 1893, George Thomas killed Town Marshal David Douglass at Bluff Springs. He was still on the lam. At his death in 1895, William Thomas was wanted for killing a deputy sheriff in Henry County.[16]

Other individuals may have been wounded or killed on suspicion of being Railroad Bill:

A gentleman from Pensacola told me this morning about a letter a negro woman there had received from her husband at Mobile. The husband wrote that he was very anxious to see his spouse, but that he could not come unless he walked and that two negroes had already been killed for "Railroad Bill" between Pensacola and Mobile.

Atlanta Constitution, August 30, 1895

13

The Death of Railroad Bill

The day William Thomas was buried in Potter's Field at Montgomery, an elderly African American man named Jack Williamson happened upon an unarmed Railroad Bill on a road near Selma. It was Saturday, August 17, 1895. Williamson was on his way to the residence of his son-in-law, Bob Howard, to eat. When the ragged, tired stranger asked for food, the kindly old gentleman took him to Howard's home.[1]

The outlaw "showed signs of going to sleep as he stood on his feet, and as the food was cooking he sat in a chair and nodded." He ate "ravenously everything that was set before him" and offered to pay, but the family refused. He then asked for a place to sleep. Williamson took him to his home, six miles west of Selma, where the outlaw fell into bed and slept several hours. Later he indicated that he wanted to stay three or four days and pulled out a roll of bills, withdrew a twenty-dollar bill, and asked Williamson to purchase rice, flour, ham, and two gallons of whiskey.[2]

The desperado asked Williamson if he knew anything about Railroad Bill. The old man said that he knew nothing. "Well, that's my name—'Railroad Bill,' Hell-a-Mile."[3]

"Well, if your name is 'Hell-a-Mile,' I don't want nuffin to do wid yer. I'se skeared of any man who'd go by sich a name as dat."[4]

"I was jis a-jokin' wid you, old man."[5]

Railroad Bill again acknowledged his identity and said that he had hidden his rifle and three pistols. He also said the law "had been after him that they got the Pratt dogs on him down in the swamps and he killed the dogs and a white man, and that he killed another white man before Christmas."[6]

Around sunset, Williamson left the house for about half an hour. When he returned, the door had been left open, and Railroad Bill was missing along with Williamson's new "Sunday suit of clothes, a new pair of shoes, and a soft snuff-colored hat." In their place, Railroad Bill had left a "pair of worn out shoes and a greasy slouched hat."[7]

Williamson followed the outlaw's footprints in the soft earth until he realized that if he caught up, he might also be killed. He proceeded to report the crime, weeping as he told officers about losing his best clothing.[8]

Selma authorities were convinced that Railroad Bill was a former resident:

It is not any credit, but it is nevertheless a fact—"Railroad Bill" and Will Barker, who, for a number of years, was brakeman on the East Tennessee, Virginia and Georgia road, are one and the same man. About five years ago he was discharged by the railroad company for being implicated in the theft of some loose meat from a car. His wife,

Helen Barker, and his sister, now reside on Bow street. So far Bill has had sense enough to stay away from Selma, but now that he is in the neighborhood he may be expected any day.

Mobile Daily Register, August 20, 1895

After Railroad Bill was at Selma, his whereabouts were mostly unknown to authorities: "From time to time vague rumors have been circulated to the effect that he had been in first one part of the country and then another, but nothing definite was known of his movements." Then, on October 20, his location was reported. An old friend from southern Alabama happened upon him and spoke with him at Mountain Creek, a community about four miles north of Verbena, about fifty miles northeast of Selma.[9] Eight days later, Railroad Bill was reported at Honey Island, Louisiana, a wilderness in the Pearl River delta near the Mississippi state line:

> Railroad Bill has several intimate acquaintances in Honey Island among the negroes, and they all say that it was he who a few days ago robbed a Syrian peddler and came near killing him. They say that Railroad Bill will be hard to capture; that he is a very desperate character, and that he is no doubt now hidden somewhere in the depths of the swamps getting his plans matured for robbing a train at the first opportunity which presents itself.

New Orleans Daily Picayune, October 28, 1895

On November 23 the desperado was seen again. William M. Johnson, an L&N employee and resident of Mobile who had once worked with Railroad Bill, saw him talking with another individual at the L&N freight depot in New Orleans. Johnson said about a month earlier he had talked with Railroad Bill, and the outlaw wanted to surrender: "he knew he could prove his innocence of the charges against him."[10]

By December 1895, Railroad Bill was back in southern Alabama, but not to surrender. He was suspected of indulging in his former lifestyle:

> Trainmen coming into Mobile from the Louisville and Nashville Railroad are of the belief that the erstwhile desperado, "Railroad Bill," is again in his old haunts in Escambia county and that he now has several associates. It is reported that when northbound freight train No. 74 reached Wilson station early yesterday morning the trainmen discovered that the seals on several cars had been broken and freight to the amount of about $500 taken from the cars. This train met and passed southbound freight train No. 71 further up the road and the crew of No. 71 report that when Hurricane Bayou was reached the seals on several cars loaded with old iron were discovered broken. As one of the brakemen examined the seals two negroes stepped from out of the darkness into the glare of the trainman's lantern and ordered him to move on, which he did. The theory is that the thieves boarded No. 74 at Hurricane Bayou and, after entering the cars threw their plunder off alongside the track. They left the train at Wilson station and boarding No. 71 returned to Hurricane Bayou to gather in the stolen property. It is highly probable that the trail after "Railroad" will be taken up where it was left off last summer.
>
> Mobile *Daily Register*, December 15, 1895

On January 1, 1896, the Atlanta *Constitution* published a report from Savannah, Georgia, stating that Railroad Bill had taken passage on a steamboat to Liberia, Africa, under an assumed name. Numerous voyages were being made by African Americans seeking new lives as colonists to the West African nation.[11] The *Constitution* noted that Railroad Bill's "identity appears to be unquestioned" and took the opportunity to reflect on the outlaw's criminal career:

> Railroad Bill was a unique character in the criminal world. He was not an ordinary murderer. He exhibited no thirst for blood. He never wrecked a train; he never harmed a woman or a child. There is no record of his ever having killed any man who was not in pursuit of him. He is quoted as having said that he was conscientious about whom he killed. His daring and physical courage were unsurpassed and the record of his adventures in The Constitution's columns in the past year will attest to his unerring aim and peculiar generalship.
>
> Atlanta *Constitution*, January 1, 1896

Authorities in southern Alabama weren't buying the Savannah story: "Those who were familiar with the negro laughed at the report and gave it no credence."[12] Any question regarding Railroad Bill's whereabouts was answered two months later by Stanley Watson, a Texas reporter for the Brenham *Evening Press*. Watson, while tramping to Tampa to take a steamship to Cuba to cover an insurrection, told authorities in Pensacola that he had shared a ride with Railroad Bill:

> [Watson] says that he had a berth on the "blind" end of the baggage car of the local passenger train from Mobile

and during a stop at a small way station between Mobile and Flomaton a negro climbed up on the seat beside him. He noticed that the negro carried a Winchester rifle and a belt full of cartridges, and asked him what he was doing with so much artillery. The man replied that he needed them for detectives, sheriffs, and other game, and asked the Texan if he had never heard of Railroad Bill—that he was the man.

Pensacola Daily News, February 21, 1896

When Railroad Bill reappeared in southern Alabama, the L&N transferred chief Detective John Harlan from Louisville to head the company's effort to bring the desperado to justice:

A change was made in the secret service department of the entire L. and N. system, the chief having accepted a position in St. Louis. The gallant Tom Watts, the man who had had so many close calls with the outlaw, was transferred to Pensacola, and Mr. Jeff Harlan put in his place here [in Montgomery], while Mr. John Harlan was appointed chief of the secret service division. All three of them were thrown into the field, though, and the hunt became pretty hot.

Montgomery Daily Advertiser, March 8, 1896

Harlan hired J. Allen Ross, an African American undercover detective, to assist in the investigation. Harlan described Ross as "a very shrewd negro politician. He was a lawyer of some ability, as well as preacher and detective and an all-around scout. He was well educated and could play his part in most any undertaking." Ross was given the task of gathering information from several people who were thought to be assisting Railroad

Bill. After organizing a series of church revivals to befriend the individuals, he learned from them where one of Railroad Bill's hideouts was located. He also learned that Henry Caldwell had recently been released from prison and "had taken Mark Stinson's place as Slater's prime minister."[13]

At the same time that railroad detectives were making progress in their investigation through Ross's efforts, civil authorities in Escambia County, Alabama, were making progress of their own. Their break came after a robbery at the home of Atmore telegraph operator George W. Humphreys on the night of February 15, 1896. The Humphreys family returned from a school event to find several articles of women's and children's clothing missing. The next day, Constable James Leonard McGowin of Atmore arrested Will Payne, a neighbor of the Humphreys, and charged him with the robbery. Payne was placed in jail at Brewton, where he pled an improbable story. According to Payne, "Railroad Bill forced him at the point of a pistol, to stand guard while Bill went in and robbed the house, after which he took to the woods." Payne told his story so earnestly that he eventually convinced McGowin and Sheriff James McMillan of his truthfulness.[14]

Payne also drew a map to lead the officers to one of Railroad Bill's hideouts. It was at "Joe Hall's old place not far from Flomaton." There, it was said, the outlaw had been routinely advised on the movements of the detectives and had "spent many of his leisure moments and had rested secure almost in sight of the road down which he had watched the posses go for the purpose of his capture."[15]

On Saturday, March 7, about a week after receiving Payne's map, McMillan, McGowin, R. J. Jopin, and Dan T. Leatherwood raided Railroad Bill's hideout. McMillan and McGowin forced entry into the cabin and found it empty of occupants. It was "well fortified for an attack, portholes being cut on all sides for the use of Bill's deadly Winchester." While they were inside, a friend of the desperado "tapped gently on the door asking admittance." The officers learned that Railroad Bill had been in Atmore for several days and had recently been barbered on the veranda of a house. The posse proceeded to Atmore, and near town they happened to see Railroad Bill at a house. They did not, however, attempt his capture. Instead, they planned to capture the desperado that night. They had received information, evidently from the person who came to the hideout (Payne had been in jail for about three weeks), that Railroad Bill would appear that night in Atmore. The officers decided "to lay for him, and if possible capture, or, failing, kill him."[16]

While some newspapers indicate that Railroad Bill had planned a robbery, the Evergreen *Courant* states that he had planned to make a purchase at a general store in town. To deceive him into believing that the posse had given up and disbanded, Sheriff McMillan took a train back to Brewton, "leaving instructions that he be wired if there were any further developments." Then, at about 9:00 p.m., McGowin and Leatherwood went to a general store in Atmore operated by proprietors Tidmore and Ward.[17]

While Sheriff McMillan's posse was making progress in Atmore, John Harlan's detectives were making progress near Perdido. Deputy Sheriff Allen Brewton—the officer who had attempted to arrest Railroad Bill for carrying a repeating rifle at Bluff Springs in 1894—arrested Henry Caldwell. Brewton, with local arrest authority, seems to have made the arrest in collaboration with Detectives Jeff Harlan and Watts. Caldwell was charged with robbing a store at McDavid, Florida, five miles south of Bluff Springs, on March 1, 1896. When taken into custody, he had cartridges stolen from the store that he was taking to Railroad Bill. The detectives transported Caldwell to John Harlan, who confronted him with the evidence that had been gathered against him. Caldwell turned state's witness and revealed that he and Railroad Bill had robbed the railroad depot at Perdido and the post office at Sullivan's Switch. He also revealed that most of the merchandise stolen in the robberies was stored in his cabin near Perdido, the one he shared with his wife, Mary.[18]

John Harlan and his detectives transported Caldwell to jail at Pensacola, where he was charged with robbing the McDavid store. The detectives then returned to the Pensacola depot to await a train to take them to Perdido to continue their investigation. But while they waited, they received startling news that Constable McGowin had killed Railroad Bill in Atmore. The killing had taken place at about 8:50 p.m., March 7, in the store operated by Tidmore and Ward.[19]

Sheriff McMillan and Superintendent McKinney exchanged telegraphic messages rapidly after receiving news of the killing. In one, McMillan beckoned McKinney to "come down and rejoice with us." In another he asked, "Can you possible [sic] get me to Atmore with switch engine? Am afraid negroes will take body away from McGowan."[20]

"Get your men ready," McKinney replied. "I will have a coach there in 30 minutes."[21]

The special train arrived in Brewton at 10:30 p.m. and was met by a crowd of people wanting additional information on the particulars of the killing. Sheriff McMillan, deputies, a reporter, and spectators boarded the train, and it took them to Flomaton, where they transferred to a faster train that had been made ready. Forty-five minutes after leaving Brewton, they arrived at Williams Station in Atmore. With lanterns lighting their way, the men walked toward the store several blocks away. As they approached, their pace increased until they were almost at a run. Someone nearby heckled, "You would be in a hurry to run the other way if you thought he was alive."[22]

Tidmore and Ward's store was in a two-story wood-framed structure. A photo published in the Atmore *Spectrum* in 1907 shows the building with a typical storefront facing the street and two doors on the left side as viewed from the street.[23] The side door closest to the street had a small overhang. It was evidently the side door through which Railroad Bill was shot. The reporter from Brewton described what he saw inside the store:

> Lying near the center of the store between the counters was the body of the negro in a pool of blood. He presented a terrible appearance, his face having been badly torn up with a load of shot, said to have been fired after he was down. He had on dirty greasy looking clothes, shoes worn through at the toes, a much-used leather belt around the waist, in which was his revolver on his right side and his Winchester on his left and down his pants leg.
>
> He lay in a pool of blood where he had fallen. After viewing the body a few minutes, the Sheriff ordered hands to carry it to the station, where it was placed in the coach and taken back to Brewton.
>
> Brewton *Standard Gauge*, March 12, 1896

Accounts of the killing varied in the press. Some differences can be explained by the fact that there were two competing factions involved in the killing, and each told the story to enhance its claim on the reward money. One faction consisted of Constable McGowin and Dan Leatherwood; the other consisted of M. C. Tidmore, R. J. Johns, and Jesse Johns. But there were conflicting reports that are not easily explained. For example, the names of the shooters varied significantly in the press. The Greenville *Advocate* named J. L. McGowin, Dan Leatherford, John Johns, and Joe Johns; the Evergreen *Courant* named McGowan, Leatherwood, and Jopin; the Pensacola *Daily News* named J. W. McGowan, D. F. Leatherwood, R. J. Johns, and R. J. Jopin; the New Orleans *Daily Picayune* named J. S. McGowin, J. R. Johns, and Joe Johns; the Philadelphia *Inquirer* named J. M. McGowan and Joseph and J. R. Johns; and the Montgomery *Daily Advertiser* named J. L. McGowan, Dan Leatherford, and John R. and Joe Johns as well as mentioning a Tob Johns. A more accurate account might be the names listed in 1901 in an act passed by the Florida legislature which authorized payment of the state's reward money: "James Leonard McGowin, R. J. Johns, Jesse Johns and M. C. Tidmore."[24]

According to the Brewton *Standard Gauge,* Railroad Bill had purchased provisions in Tidmore and Ward's store two weeks before he was killed. On the day of the killing, M. C. Tidmore knew that the desperado was back in town and expected him to return to the store, apparently around closing time. Some reports indicate that McGowin and Leatherwood were surprised to find Railroad Bill at the store, but the Evergreen *Courant* stated that the posse had received information that the outlaw "would seek to replenish his exhausted larder." Bob Ebron—probably the person who came to the hideout near Flomaton—was eventually identified as the source of the information:

[Railroad Bill] was betrayed by a negro named Bob Ebron, who learned that the fugitive had ordered a gallon of whisky to be sent to an Atmore store for him. It was to come to the supply firm of Tidmore and Ward and being notified that the negro was expected to come after the whisky that night, two men were placed in the store and one or two were watching outside the building.

Birmingham News-Age Herald, March 11, 1928

The four men mentioned in this quotation were R. J. Johns and Jesse Johns inside the store and Leonard McGowin and Dan Leatherwood outside the store. The two pairs were not, however, working together. R. J. Johns and Jesse Johns were working with Tidmore, who would "decoy [Railroad Bill] into his store, and have him shot by two men in hiding." In preparation, Tidmore "closed his front door, leaving the side door open." His plan was for the outlaw to enter by the side door, and at an appropriate time he would give a signal for R. J. Johns and Jesse Johns to draw their weapons and fire on the unsuspecting desperado. The shooters were probably arranged to catch Railroad Bill in a crossfire that would force him toward the middle of the room and away from the side exit. But if he reached the front door, it would be locked, hindering his exit. At the same time, a locked door would prevent a bystander from entering just before the fusillade began.[25]

Railroad Bill came to the store a little before 9:00 p.m. and took a seat on a wooden barrel. From that position he could probably watch the people inside the room as well as the front door. He was traveling somewhat incognito; his appearance had changed after being barbered, probably removing an overgrown beard. His most distinguishing characteristic, his large-bore .44-caliber Winchester rifle, which he typically carried by a homemade shoulder strap, was out of sight. He had inserted it inside the left leg of his pantaloons. It would have caused him to limp, and that too may have contributed to his disguise. Any portion of the rifle protruding above his pantaloons would have been hidden by an overcoat that he probably wore in early March. The coat would also have covered a pair of .44-caliber Colt revolvers that he had tucked inside a cartridge belt strapped around his waist. According to the Evergreen *Courant*, "not carrying any visible implements of war, at first cast a shadow of doubt on his identity, but one of the posse having come into close conflict with him before, knew him the instant he exposed his face to the light, and the whole of the party, advancing to a point where his features were fully visible, knew him as the famous desperado."[26]

Railroad Bill had undoubtedly planned on Caldwell arriving that day to deliver the cartridges taken from the McDavid store. But with Caldwell in custody, he was not available to assist the outlaw by purchasing the whiskey or by casing the store before Railroad Bill entered. Consequently, the notorious outlaw boldly entered the store alone. Either he was deceived into believing the sheriff's posse had disbanded, or as the Mobile *Daily Register* noted, he was "a desperado, pure and simple, enamored of his own recklessness."[27]

The Brewton *Standard Gauge* published McGowin's version of the killing:

After seeing Railroad in the evening [McGowin] thought he would visit the store at night. So he rode up in the vicinity of the store and hitched his horse. After some minutes he took his rifle and went towards the store. The front door being shut he walked past the side door and looked in. There were several people inside, and things were resting easy. Mr. Leatherwood who was working with Mr. McGowin went into the store on a pretext of buying something, but really to see Railroad. Mr. Mc-Gowin walked back by the door and got a fair view of Railroad, at his back, and he took deliberate aim from without the door and fired, bringing Railroad to the floor. He then stepped in the door and fired again and retreated. Immediately there was considerable firing by Leatherwood and the Johns. McGowin supposing Railroad was doing some of the shooting thought he would run out the door, and that he would have another shot at him as he came out.

Brewton *Standard Gauge*, March 12, 1896

McGowin's life may have been saved by "the front door being shut." If the town's policeman had entered with a Winchester in hand, Railroad Bill would have noticed, and one can only speculate on what may have occurred. Instead, with the door apparently locked, McGowin went to the side door and recognized his old nemesis. Leatherwood then entered on the "pretext of buying something, but really to see Railroad." With positive identification, McGowin fired at near point-blank range at the back of the desperado. His .32-caliber Winchester rifle, however, fired small bullets that were probably insufficient in mass to immediately bring "Railroad to the floor," as the Brewton *Standard Gauge* indicated.[28]

Tidmore, before McGowin fired the first shot, had been unable to signal for his men to start their fusillade. R. J. Johns had ventured across the room, leaving his shotgun out of sight behind a cider barrel:

> [He] found himself some distance from his trusty gun, and so as not to arouse the negro's suspicions the young man had recourse to stratagem and, pretending to be under the influence of liquor, reeled toward the place where his gun stood, and when he could get it up to his shoulder he did not take any chances but fired at once, the load tearing the head almost from the body, and then, as he was about to fall, another of the posse shot him full in front in the breast. The negro fell and as he fell his hand went to his side where he had his pistol, when the third man of the posse fired, shooting the hand of the negro, almost severing it at the wrist and making it useless. Bill, mortally wounded, survived only a moment: he breathed his last and then the people about, realizing that their old enemy was no more to trouble them, set up a shout which was heard for some distance away.
>
> New Orleans *Times-Democrat*, March 9, 1896

This article makes no mention of McGowin's involvement in the killing, which would have increased the constable's claim on the reward money. A similar but contradictory account, attributed to R. J. Johns, appeared in the Brewton *Standard Gauge*. It stated that R. J. Johns "was drawing some cider from a barrel where he had his gun hid, and that at an agreed signal from Mr. Tidmore he shot Railroad, bringing him to the floor, and that he then fired the other barrel into him."[29]

A likely scenario that emerges from published reports is that McGowin initiated the fusillade. He fired a shot from outside the doorway, cocked his Winchester, and fired again after stepping through the threshold. He then stepped out of the doorway as firing continued by men inside the store. The first of those shots was by R. J. Johns, who had raised his shotgun from behind the cider barrel and fired at the head of Railroad Bill. That blast mangled the outlaw's face, neck, and shoulder. Leatherwood and Jesse Johns, the only men using revolvers, then fired a succession of pistol shots. One of their shots struck Railroad Bill in the chest. As he staggered toward the middle of the room and fell, he reached his right hand across his body to grasp a pistol tucked inside his belt. Another pistol shot struck that hand, "almost severing it at the wrist and making it useless." Either that shot or another "broke the trigger finger of his right hand just as it closed on the butt of the pistol" and broke the grip of the pistol. While Railroad Bill was on the floor, he received a second blast from R. J. Johns's shotgun, and "the words which the outlaw had commenced to address to the storekeeper died on his lips." Realizing that their enemy had perished, the men in the store raised a shout.[30]

Buttons, bullets, and pieces of Railroad Bill's clothing were taken for souvenirs. Additional cartridges, including a handkerchief wrapped around even more cartridges, were found in his pockets, "the entire supply being sufficient to have carried on a battle for many hours."[31]

As news of Railroad Bill's death spread across the nation in newspapers, a relative of Stanley Watson made an inquiry from Texas:

Special Officer A. G. Gordon, of the police force, received a letter this morning from John Watson, a nurseryman at Brenham, Tex., inquiring if his brother, Stanley Watson, was not entitled to a portion of the reward offered for Railroad Bill. Stanley Watson is the "hobo" correspondent of the Brenham paper and readers of THE NEWS will remember an interview with him, published in these columns about three weeks since, in which he described a meeting with the outlaw while "beating" his way on a train from Mobile to Pensacola.

Pensacola *Daily News,* March 16, 1896

The Texas inquiry received little recognition, but claims made by the two factions involved in the killing were given a hearing before a committee of arbitration convened at Brewton by John Harlan. In addition to the standing reward of $1,250, the L&N offered a lifetime pass on the company's railway. The committee decided to divide the money equally between the two factions and to award the lifetime pass to McGowin. Tidmore, however, soon experienced a change of heart and asked that his portion be given to R. J. Johns and Jesse Johns.[32]

It would be another five years before the Florida legislature approved payment of the state's portion of the reward by passing "An Act to Authorize the Payment of Two Hundred Dollars, the Reward Offered by the Governor of Florida, for the Capture of the Outlaw Morris Slater." Thus the saga of Railroad Bill began and ended with acts by Florida's legislature. The first required a permit to carry a repeating rifle in public; the second authorized payment for killing a person who refused.[33] Robert Brooks wrote:

> Much of the later career of Slater as an outlaw began with his owning, and shooting a .22-calibre rifle, and Florida having a law about licensing, or taxing, Winchester rifles. Differences arose, bad blood was engendered, and before the chapter had ended "Railroad Bill" had killed two or

three men at least, and many believe that he killed at least four or five.

Birmingham *News-Age Herald*, March 11, 1928

The Mobile *Daily Register* added an interesting footnote to the death of Railroad Bill:

Prognosticators have been averring for many months that sooner or later the daring desperado, Railroad Bill, would turn up his toes and that when this interesting event occurred he would "die with his boots on." But it would have required some modern system of projection equal to the Cathode ray to have prognosticated that Bill would meet his death on the anniversary of his first appearance in public print. This singular coincidence was noted by a staff man of The Register this morning. On March 6, 1895—one year from yesterday—as will be seen by the above report, the fusillade between the negro outlaw and a Louisville and Nashville train crew occurred near Hurricane Bayou. The following day Bill became an object of interest to the press of three states and since that time his movements have been of absorbing interest.

Mobile *Daily Register*, March 8, 1896

14

A Morbid Business

The night Railroad Bill was killed, his body was transported on a special train provided by Superintendent McKinney. The body arrived in Brewton about 3:00 a.m. on Sunday, March 8, 1896, and was taken to a packing shed and placed on a table where hundreds of people came to see the "ghastly scene."[1]

About 9:00 a.m. the body was moved to a private room for Dr. Louis M. McLendon, a local physician, to conduct a postmortem. He counted fifteen gunshot wounds in the body. The right side of the face and the right hand were mangled, and the index finger on the right hand was broken.[2]

A description of Railroad Bill published two months before his death stated that "the thumb on one hand is missing." No mention of the thumb is made in Dr. McLendon's autopsy, but a photograph of Railroad Bill in death clearly shows the left hand fully intact. The right hand is less distinct, but four fingers can be distinguished with the index finger seemingly bandaged, which would be consistent with having been broken in the fusillade and wrapped while the body was being embalmed. The thumb on that hand is not obvious in the photograph. John Harlan remarked that "part of 'Railroad Bill's' right hand was blown away with buckshot." He may have assumed that the missing thumb on the mangled hand had been severed in the fusillade, but apparently it was missing long before the outlaw was killed.[3]

Dr. McLendon discovered two earlier wounds in the right hand of the body with projectiles still buried beneath the skin. The Montgomery *Daily Advertiser* attributed those to Dr. O'Bannon's shotgun when he fired on Railroad Bill at Bluff Springs. But the desperado had also faced shotguns in the hands of Deputy Sheriff Brewton at Bluff Springs, trainmen at Hurricane Bayou, Detective Watts at Stewart's barn, and possibly moonshiners in Baldwin County.[4]

Undertaker John G. Wood traveled from Pensacola to Brewton to embalm the body. After the autopsy, he stitched the mouth and the right hand and dressed the body in a dark funeral suit with no shoes, probably because the original shoes were worn through to the toes. He noted that Railroad Bill was "as prettily proportioned as any man he ever saw."[5]

The corpse was taken to an open area and photographed. Constable McGowin stood beside the body, holding the Winchester Model 1873 rifle that he had used in Tidmore and Ward's store. Railroad Bill's Winchester rested alongside his body. But the inscription "R. R. Bill" carved into the stock was not apparent in the photograph, and neither was damage to the butt of the rifle, which was "splintered where it was struck by a ball." A revolver lay in Railroad Bill's lap with its grip missing, having been shot away during the barrage.[6]

After being placed in a metal casket, the corpse was shipped to Montgomery by train for official identification. Authorities at Brewton were convinced that the body was "Bill beyond any possible doubt." Facial scars, frostbitten toes, and physical characteristics matched published descriptions of the outlaw. Trainmen who knew the desperado "recognized him instantly as their old enemy." Sampson Sherrill, who had talked at length with Railroad Bill at the Foshee farm, said it was the same man. The McMillan brothers thought it was their old nemesis and published a note of thanks to those who had helped bring the outlaw to his end. They also asked for "any information from white or colored regarding his past life and his papers and belongings that are in the possession of someone—anything that will throw light on his daring career."[7]

The corpse arrived at Union Station in Montgomery at 5:30 p.m. on Saturday, March 9. It had been taken there for "the purpose of satisfying the authorities of the state and the Louisville and Nashville railroad as to its identity, so as to facilitate the collection of the rewards offered."[8] When the coffin was opened,

> There was a perfect mob of curious people at the depot to see it, but scant gratification was given their curiosity, for the crowd became so enormous that the top had to be replaced on the coffin, which was put in the baggage room and admittance denied.
>
> Montgomery *Daily Advertiser*, March 10, 1896

With the body locked out of public view, an enterprising scheme was imposed, probably the next day, to make it available "to the curious public at 25 cents a look." Something similar had been proposed for Rube Burrow's body when "several parties in [Birmingham] wired the family offers of a large sum for the body, which they wanted to embalm and place on exhibition, but the offers were all refused."[9]

In Railroad Bill's case, no family member claimed the corpse, and it seems to have become ex officio property of the officers accompanying it. But in realizing that profit could be generated, the casket was taken to an empty freight car near the station and opened for viewing by paying patrons.[10] The morbid practice soon drew criticism:

> It can be said to the credit of the community that comparatively few people paid an admission price of 25 cents to see the corpse of William, and it may be also remarked that such a sight could only appeal to people of morbid tastes and perverted sensibilities.
>
> Such a proceeding has been roundly condemned on all sides as being barbarous, and if the men in charge of the body think that by showing it in this manner the exhibition will serve as a terrible example to an ignorant and vicious class from which "Railroad Bill's" are developed, they are far wrong. Morris Slater, in the minds of this class, is already considered something of a hero, and now the effect in this respect is being strengthened.
>
> But primarily, the public exhibition of the body is intended as a money-making scheme, and upon this score the practice deserves to be condemned, for it is an outrage upon a civilized community.
>
> The public has had enough of Railroad Bill; he paid the penalty of his crimes and should be buried, for after all he was a human being.
>
> Montgomery *Daily Advertiser*, March 13, 1896

Officials in Montgomery forbade the practice, and on Friday, March 13, Sheriff McMillan and Deputy Sheriff Railey transferred the body to Pensacola for official identification to receive the reward offered by Florida's governor. On arrival, it was met by "an immense crowd of people, principally colored, [who] had gathered at the union depot to catch a glimpse of the body, but a force of policemen was on hand and good order was preserved."[11]

Several people who had known Railroad Bill examined the corpse and verified its identity for Sheriff Smith to communicate to Governor Henry L. Mitchell. It was then moved to the undertaker's office of Northup and Wood, where John Wood found it "in a perfect state of preservation." George W. Turton was scheduled to take photographs, but it is unclear if any of his photographs have survived. The photograph taken at Brewton, however, was being marketed: "Photos of the Desperado as he appeared after death for FIFTY CENTS. Per cent goes to children of the deceased Sheriff."[12]

The body was transferred to Palmetto Beach on Pensacola Bay and placed on display in Armory Hall for the paying public to see. To accommodate those wishing to see the body, a notice appeared in the Pensacola *Daily News* stating that "beginning at 10:30 a.m. trains will be run to Palmetto Beach every hour during to-day and to-morrow." But again the morbid practice met stiff criticism and was prohibited. With Sheriff McMillan having traveled to Brewton and Constable McGowin having traveled to Defuniak Spring, Florida, Deputy Sheriff Railey of Brewton remained in charge of the body.[13] He accompanied it to Mobile on Monday, March 16, arriving at 1:40 p.m.:

No sooner had the body arrived than Officers Roy Hoyle and George Curry informed Mr. Railey that he could not exhibit the body in Mobile. Pretty soon after the train arrived, Chief Burke, accompanied by Special Officers [Edward] Morris and [Thomas] McGovern, came down to the depot, and the chief sought Mr. Railey and informed him that the mayor [Constantine L. Lavretta] had issued an order to the effect that the exhibition of the remains of the dead negro should not be allowed in this city.

Mobile *Daily Register*, March 17, 1896

Within twenty minutes of arriving in the city, the body, "enclosed in a metallic casket, which in turn was covered by a wooden box," was placed on a train to Birmingham. The plan was to have it "embalmed by Major Jack Miller's petrifying process" in Birmingham. The apparent intent was to market a fully preserved corpse for extended exhibition as a curiosity.[14]

Kate Leigh McMillan, whose husband, Edward, was killed by Railroad Bill, was a critic of the scheme to commercialize the body, particularly the implication that she and her children were benefiting monetarily:

I have seen extracts in different papers to the effect that the dead body of Railroad Bill was being exhibited at different points, charges made for the same, and that the proceeds were to be given to the family of the late Sheriff E. S. McMillan.

Please state through your columns that such proceedings were not only unauthorized by, but were unknown to me; that I have not, and would not, accept one single cent derived from the exhibition of the body of the murderer of my husband.

Pensacola *Daily News*, March 29, 1896

The body seemed destined for indefinite exhibition, but in a surprising turn of events, it was transferred back to Pensacola and laid to rest in the African American section of St. John's Cemetery, a public cemetery founded by the Masons in 1876. The casket was opened, the rifle and pistol that had been traveling with the body were removed, and in a ceremony witnessed by Pensacola's mayor, W. E. Anderson, the body was laid to rest.[15] According to a Brewton newspaper:

> The curtain has been rung down on the thrilling tragedy of "Railroad Bill." The last act in this now famous tragedy took place in Pensacola yesterday afternoon when the mortal remains of the noted desperado were laid to rest in the cemetery there in the presence of Undertaker Wood and Mayor Anderson of the city of Pensacola. During his eventful life "Railroad" received distinguished attention from many citizens in high places. For more than a year every sheriff in the South Alabama and West Florida was unduly solicitous about his health and whereabouts, and when sheriffs were present to soothe the agonies of final dissolution, and it was only fitting that his funeral should be accorded official recognition.
>
> Brewton *Standard Gauge*, April 2, 1896

But how did the body come to be saved from further commercial exploitation? As the Atlanta *Constitution* surmised, "the managers of old desperado's lifeless clay finally despaired when they reached Pensacola and consigned it as stated to the ground from whence it sprung." The grave remained unmarked until 2012 when the Friends of the St. Johns Cemetery Foundation, at the request of the author, located documentation that identified the site. The author's wife benevolently provided a headstone that now marks the last resting place for Railroad Bill.[16]

Conclusion

Endless Folklore

Carl Carmer described Railroad Bill as "a god of negro mythology."[1] But there was nothing mythological about the outlaw's astounding ability to escape capture. He escaped a gunfight at Bluff Springs, escaped being locked in a freight car at Hurricane Bayou, escaped a posse after the Stewart and Wright incident, escaped a gunfight at Hurricane Bayou, escaped a gunfight on a wagon road near Bay Minette, escaped a gunfight at Stewart's barn, escaped a detectives' posse at Pollard, escaped detectives at Stockton, escaped a detectives' posse at Mount Vernon, escaped a sheriffs' posse north of Mount Vernon, escaped a posse at Molino, escaped a posse at Bluff Springs, escaped multiple posses in the panhandle after killing Sheriff McMillan, escaped Duckworth's posse on the Mississippi coast, escaped a railroad posse at Wolf River, escaped a posse's assault on a hideout at Honeycut Creek, and escaped scores of men with bloodhounds for five days in the swamps between Brewton and Castleberry. His record of inexplicable escapes encouraged a Montgomery editor to write:

> The entire detective system of the Louisville and Nashville Railroad Company was drawn into the hunt for the negro. A number of the most skillful of the picked men of Pinkerton detective agency exhausted their cunning. Hundreds of volunteer citizens from the Counties of Butler, Crenshaw, Conecuh, Escambia, Baldwin and Mobile in Alabama and Escambia and other districts of North Florida, together with the law officers did all that in their power lay and, baffled, gave up the chase through sheer weariness.
>
> Montgomery *Advertiser*, December 17, 1905

Railroad Bill's talent for survival gave rise to fantastic stories purporting that he had a supernatural ability to confound his pursuers by disappearing or conjuring into an animal or turning into an inanimate object.[2]

At the end of the Castleberry chase, two Montgomery reporters visited Brewton and commented on the stories circulating about town at that time:

> [Railroad Bill] is like the Phoenix—he can not be downed and rises from the ashes with all imaginable sang froid. . . . [S]ome white people who should know better, not only repeat these impossible bogy tales with great gusto, but actually believe them. This class of people are firmly convinced that Railroad Bill has the superhuman power of easily transforming himself into any object, animate or inanimate, that he wants to.
>
> Montgomery *Daily Advertiser*, August 7, 1895

Mrs. Ahren, proprietor of the Ahren House Hotel in Brewton, told reporters that she had greeted her washerwoman the previous day with a question that had come into vogue around Brewton: "Well, Aunt Rachael, have you, too, seen Railroad Bill?"[3]

The kindly washerwoman replied that the outlaw had come to her door Wednesday night, saying he was "powerful hungry" and asking for something to eat. She retrieved food for him, but she said he turned into an "old cow jess as quick as I turned my back."[4]

According to Mrs. Ahren, the elderly lady "seemed to believe this wild creature of her own imagination as firmly as I am standing here, and I know I simply pretended to take it all in."[5]

Not all stories of the supernatural came from people claiming to believe them. Mr. Padgen, "one of the most distinguished men in that part of the country,"[6] told the reporters one such story:

The negroes had been telling so many of those marvelous tales about Railroad's changing his form at will that it was getting monotonous. The other night I was on a stand up near the canning factory having with me an illiterate, superstitious kind of fellow. The night was a beautiful moonlight one, as bright as day, and we were about fifty yards from the railroad track. Everything was as still and deserted as a graveyard, when, about 12 o'clock, an old white dog trotted down the track towards the depot. In about thirty minutes here came the same old dog trotting back up the track, and as soon as I saw it an idea struck me. Calling the "Pinkerton" who was with me I said, "As sure as we are standing here, that dog was Railroad

Bill—he has been down to the telegraph office, got the program for tomorrow and all the other news he could pick up, and is going back into those woods, change into a man again and move on." The woods I pointed to were about 200 yards from where we were standing—within easy rifle range—and when I said that you should have seen my companion. He jumped as if he was shot, turned white as a sheet, and, with clattering teeth, said, "I think I had better go down to the depot and tell the operator about it." Off he went on a dead run down the track, and that was the last seen of him that night.

Montgomery Daily Advertiser, August 7, 1895

As a boy, Edward Leigh McMillan was told a story of the supernatural. He vividly remembered an African American woman telling him "that she saw a man she thought to be 'Railroad Bill' coming down the road one afternoon just at dusk, and just before he reached her he changed into a sheep."[7]

McMillan maintained a lifelong interest in the story of Railroad Bill and sought information from numerous sources, including Andrew Cunningham and Leonard McGowin. McMillan believed the outlaw had invented many of the "stories of adventure and wonderful powers in order to make the negroes afraid not to render him assistance and shelter." He said that since Railroad Bill "was looked upon in the light of a hero," it was easy for him to sow the stories of mystique that proliferated around Brewton. That assessment seems to be corroborated by the Montgomery Daily Advertiser on April 10, 1895. It stated that individuals harboring Railroad Bill in Baldwin County "are afraid of him and seem to look upon him as something inhuman, they believe that his life is bewitched, and this superstition serves the purpose of defeating our plans for capturing him."[8]

It is difficult perhaps for someone in the twenty-first century to fully appreciate the value of mythological stories to nineteenth-century society. But the same individual would probably have little difficulty acknowledging the value of mythological stories portrayed by twenty-first-century entertainment media. The enormous profits generated are evidence of value. But regarding mythological stories in nineteenth-century culture, the *Atlantic Monthly* wrote in 1895, "the Afro-American is quite aware that 'white folks' laugh at his notions, and this knowledge has fostered in him a secretiveness concerning his inner thoughts. . . . [T]here is something in heaven and earth not dreamed of in the white man's philosophy."[9]

A newspaper editor named W. W. Screws published the first twentieth-century attempt to tell the full story of Railroad Bill. This lengthy article, which appeared in the Montgomery *Advertiser* in 1905, was titled "The Making and Undoing of an Outlaw: A Thrilling Narrative of the Rise and Fall of a Negro Desperado." Unfortunately, he chose to write a highly fictionalized work, expanding, for example, Railroad Bill's criminal career from two to four years, the number of victims from two to four, and the number of wounded to "scores of white men." In 1927, John B. Harlan attempted a factual account but introduced numerous errors that were subsequently recounted by various authors. Historian James Penick commented that Harlan's article "became standard for writers with scholarly pretensions in need of a quick summary of Railroad Bill's story." In 1934, Carl Carmer wrote *Stars Fell on Alabama* and included a section about Railroad Bill. The literary success of his work brought Railroad Bill's legacy to national attention. Several academic articles followed, including those by Margaret Figh in 1937, R.L. Scribner in 1949, Carolyn McLendon in 1977, John Roberts in 1981, James Penick in 1994, and Burgin Mathews in 2003. Norm Cohen in 2000 dedicated a chapter to Railroad Bill in *Long Steel Rail: The Railroad in American Folksong.*[10]

The legacy of the outlaw was promoted most, however, by the lyrics of a folk ballad. The first published "Railroad Bill" lyrics appeared in the Atlanta *Constitution* on August 18, 1895, during Railroad Bill's criminal career. They were included in a section of the paper titled "A Sunday Symphony":

"Railroad Bill" was an outlaw bold,
 And he'd swing you to a limb,
 Or cut your throat for a dollar note,
 Or a pair of shoes, or an overcoat;
 So a prize was out for him.
And they scoured the country far and near;
 If a fellow tapped a till
 And skipped with a dollar,
 You'd hear 'em holler:
 "We've got him! 'Railroad Bill!'"
And day by day, while he wanders free—
 Takes the country in at will,
 Detectives shout
 As they prance about:
 "We've got him! 'Railroad Bill!'"
No petty thief in the land's secure,
 With the people howling still
 To the startled town,
 As they hold him down:
 "We've got him! 'Railroad Bill!'"

          Atlanta *Constitution*, August 18, 1895

Two years after the outlaw's death, "Railroad Bill" was still being sung:

> A negro girl who is called "Baby," and who is thirty years old and weighs 170 pounds, was up before Judge Andy at the instigation of another negro woman, who claimed she had been insulted by the "Baby."
>
> "Now, you hear dis chile," said the "Baby," as she tossed her head back and rolled her eyes, "dis 'oman is mad wid me fur nuttin', and all I ever did wus to sing a song called 'Railroad Bill' in front of her house, and dat song is nice enough fur de opery house."
>
> As there was a warrant out for the "Baby," Judge Andy told her she could sing "Railroad Bill" some more if she wanted to.
>
> Atlanta *Constitution*, October 13, 1898

Howard W. Odum, a folklorist, regarded songs like "Railroad Bill" as folk poetry. In his 1911 article titled "Folk-Song and Folk-Poetry as Found in the Secular Songs of the Southern Negroes," he quotes Dr. John Meier's definition of "negro folksongs" as a type of "folk-poetry which, from whatever source and for whatever reason, has passed into the possession of the folk, the common people, so completely that each singer or reciter feels the piece to be his own." Odum observes that the performer "alters or sings ['Railroad Bill'] according to his own thoughts and feelings." And, "after the theme is once in the mouth of the singer, it matters little what the song is. The effort is to sing something about 'Bill,' and to make this conform to the general idea; and at the same time it must rhyme."[11] In his article, Odum provides the first five stanzas of a version of "Railroad Bill":

> Some one went home an' tole my wife
> All about—well, my pas' life,
> *It was that bad Railroad Bill.*
> Railroad Bill, Railroad Bill,
> He never work, an' he never will,
> *Well, it's that bad Railroad Bill.*
> Railroad Bill so mean an' so bad,
> Till he tuk ev'ything that farmer had,
> *It's that bad Railroad Bill.*
> I'm goin' home an' tell my wife,
> Railroad Bill try to take my life,
> *It's that bad Railroad Bill.*
> Railroad Bill so desp'rate an' so bad,
> He take ev'ything po' womens had,
> *An' it's that bad Railroad Bill.*[12]

Robert Winslow Gordon also collected early versions of "Railroad Bill" lyrics, most of which are now archived in the American Folklife Center of the Library of Congress. A version given to Gordon by an anonymous donor, probably in the 1930s, is as follows:

> Railroad Bill, Railroad Bill,
> H[e] never worked an' he never will,
> Well, it's bad Railroad Bill.
> Railroad Bill, Railroad Bill,
> Took ev'thing that th' farmer had;
> That bad Railroad Bill.

Kill me a chicken, send me a wing,
They think I am working but ain't done a thing,
    Then it's ride, ride, ride, ride,
Railroad Bill desperate an' bad
Take ev'thing po' women had
    Then ride, ride, ride, ride.
I am going home and tell my wife
Railroad Bill try to take my life
    Well it's bad Railroad Bill.
Railroad Bill mighty bad coon
Kill MacMillan by the light o' de moon
    Then ride, ride, ride, ride.
MacMillan had a special train,
When he got there it was spring
    Well it's ride, ride, ride, ride.
Baby baby you needn't fret,
I ain't a fool about you yet.
    Well it's ride, ride, ride, ride.
Two policemen dressed in blue
Come down de street in two and two
    Well it's looking for Railroad Bill.
Ev'body tol' him he better turn back
Bill was again down d[e] railroad track
    Well it's ride, ride, ride.[13]

In 1936, John A. Lomax, who served as curator of folklore for the Library of Congress, published an article titled "In Creation of Southern Folk Songs White Man Must Yield Palm to Colored Race." Lomax noted that African American ballads like "Railroad Bill" traditionally had practical as well as entertainment value:

The Negro has always sung in unison with his work, especially in gang labor. The wilderness of the south, with its swamps, forests and river bottoms, has been made habitable to the accompaniment of song. . . . Sometimes the meter of their ballads of negro bad men and women— Ella Speed, Frankie and Johnnie, Stagolee, Railroad Bill and others—is adapted to the movement of their labor. The songs seem to make their work easier.

Atlanta Constitution, March 8, 1936

Several performers recorded "Railroad Bill" for commercial distribution, beginning in the 1920s. They included Riley Puckett in 1924, Roba Stanley in 1924, Will Bennett in 1929, Otis Mote in 1929, and Frank Hutchison in 1929. The practice has continued with numerous other professional performers.[14]

In the mid-1950s, England enjoyed a skiffle movement promoted in part by the popularity of a rendition of "Railroad Bill" by the English musician Lonnie Donegan—the "King of Skiffle." That decade of music influenced numerous budding British artists who would make a professional mark in the 1960s. The most notable were John Lennon and Paul McCartney, who made entertainment history by becoming two of the world's most popular musicians. On the day they met, Lennon was singing "Railroad Bill."[15]

Notes

Introduction: Alabama's Bad Man

1. Liverpool *Echo*, July 5, 2007.

2. Ibid.; Atlanta *Constitution*, August 18, 1895.

3. Montgomery *Daily Advertiser*, April 10, 1895; Atmore *Advance*, December 3, 1931.

4. Fort Worth *Gazette*, February 18, 1892; Mobile *Daily Register*, May 25, May 28, 1893; New Orleans *Daily Picayune*, May 24, May 27, 1893; Atmore *Advance*, December 3, 1931; Atlanta *Constitution*, March 10, 1895.

5. Montgomery *Daily Advertiser*, March 7, July 13, 1895; Atlanta *Constitution*, April 16, 1895; Pensacola *Daily News*, July 13, 1895.

6. Harlan, "Railroad Bill," 31.

7. Brewton *Pine Belt News*, August 6, 1895; Potter, *Brief History of Escambia County, Alabama*, 10; Montgomery *Daily Advertiser*, August 7, 1895; Atlanta *Constitution*, August 18, 1895; Odum, "Folk-Song and Folk-Poetry," 289; Cohen, *Long Steel Rail*, 127.

8. State of Alabama, *Acts of the General Assembly of Alabama*, 1894–5, 161.

Chapter 1. An Eyewitness Interview

1. Montgomery *Daily Advertiser*, April 10, July 6, 1895; Mobile *Daily Register*, August 20, 1895, March 10, 1896; Birmingham *News–Age Herald*, March 11, 1928; Penick, "Railroad Bill," 85.

2. Birmingham *News–Age Herald*, March 11, 1928.

3. *Eastern Shore Courier* (Fairhope, Ala.), June 27, 1977.

4. Ibid.

5. Atlanta *Constitution*, March 8, 1896; Brewton *Pine Belt News*, March 10, 1896.

6. *Eastern Shore Courier*, June 27, 1977.

7. Ibid.

8. Ibid.

9. Montgomery *Daily Advertiser*, March 7, 1895.

10. *Eastern Shore Courier*, June 27, 1977.

11. Ibid.

12. Ibid.

13. Ibid.

14. Ibid.

15. Ibid.

16. Ibid.

17. Ibid.

18. Montgomery *Daily Advertiser*, March 12, 1895.

Chapter 2. Circus Performer

1. Montgomery *Daily Advertiser*, April 10, 1895; New Orleans *Daily Picayune*, July 10, 1895.

2. Montgomery *Daily Advertiser*, April 10, 1895; New Orleans *Daily Picayune*, April 25, 1896.

3. See *Mobile City Directory*, 1882–95; Pensacola *Daily News* July 9, September 5, 1890; Fort Worth *Gazette*, February 18, 1892; Atmore *Advance*, December 3, 1931; New Orleans *Daily Picayune*, April 26, 1896.

4. New Orleans *Daily Picayune*, July 10, 1895; Montgomery *Daily Advertiser*, April 10, 1895.

5. Pensacola *Daily News*, March 9, 1896.

6. Montgomery *Daily Advertiser*, July 6, 1895; Columbus *Enquirer-Sun*, October 24, 1890.

7. Mobile *Daily Register*, August 23, 1894, January 27, 1895, March 8, 1896.

8. W. B. Dinwiddie to R. W. Gordon, September 21, 1929, Gordon MS 782, Robert W. Gordon Manuscript Collection, American Folklife Center, Library of Congress, Washington, D.C.

9. New Orleans *Daily Picayune*, October 29, 1894; Mobile *Daily Register*, October 30, 1894.

10. Rube Burrow was also sometimes referred to in the press as Rube Burrows; Montgomery *Daily Advertiser*, March 12, April 10, 1895; Mobile *Daily Register*, April 9, 1895; Pensacola *Daily News*, April 9, 1895.

11. Eighteen years of age eighteen years ago equals age thirty-six; Montgomery *Daily Advertiser*, April 11, 1895.

12. Frederick *News*, March 10, 1896; Altoona *Mirror*, March 10, 1896.

13. Birmingham *Age-Herald*, August 18, 1895; Mobile *Daily Register*, August 20, 1895; New Orleans *Times-Democrat*, March 8, 1896.

Chapter 3. Trouble on the Railroad

1. Agee, *Rube Burrow*, 194.

2. Montgomery *Daily Advertiser*, April 10, 1895.

3. Flynt, "Tramp and the Railroads," 258, 263–65; Rezneck, "Unemployment, Unrest, and Relief," 327; New Orleans *Daily Picayune*, December 7, 1894.

4. Atlanta *Constitution*, October 17, 1897.

5. Roberts, "'Railroad Bill' and the American Outlaw Tradition," 318, 315–28.

6. Edward Leigh McMillan to R. W. Gordon, October 12, 1927, Gordon MS 3442, Robert W. Gordon Manuscript Collection, American Folklife Center, Library of Congress, Washington, D.C.; Montgomery *Daily Advertiser*, March 7, 1895.

Chapter 4. The Desperado Wyatt Tate

1. Monroeville *Journal*, March 29, 1894.

2. Ibid.; Mobile *Daily Register*, April 5, 1894.

3. Mobile *Daily Register*, April 5, 1894.

4. Mobile *Daily Register*, April 5, April 6, 1894.

5. Mobile *Daily Register*, April 6, 1894.

6. Mobile *Daily Register*, April 5, April 7, 1894.

7. Mobile *Daily Register*, April 7, 1894; Brewton *Standard Gauge*, May 17, 1894.

8. Mobile *Daily Register*, May 5, 1894; New York *Times*, May 6, 1894; Monroe *Journal*, May 10, 1894.

9. Atlanta *Constitution*, May 13, 1894; Mobile *Daily Register*, May 15, 1894; Monroe *Journal*, May 17, 1894; Brewton *Standard Gauge*, May 17, May 24, 1894. The Monroe *Journal*, May 31, 1894, corrected its May 17 report, this time calling the Marshall residence a "House of Mourning" for a departed relative.

10. Monroe *Journal*, May 17, 1894; Brewton *Standard Gauge*, May 24, 1894; Mobile *Daily Register*, May 13, 1894.

Chapter 5. The Murder of Marshal Douglass

1. New Orleans *Daily Picayune,* October 29, 1894; Atlanta *Constitution,* April 16, 1895.

2. New Orleans *Daily Picayune,* September 23, 1893; Mobile *Daily Register,* May 25, 1893.

3. New Orleans *Daily Picayune,* September 23, 1893; Mobile *Daily Register,* May 25, 1893; Washington *Post,* May 25, 1893.

4. Mobile *Daily Register,* May 25, 1893; New Orleans *Daily Picayune,* September 23, 1893.

5. New Orleans *Daily Picayune,* September 23, 1893; Mobile *Daily Register,* May 25, 1893.

6. Mobile *Daily Register,* May 25, 1893; New Orleans *Daily Picayune,* September 23, 1893.

7. Mobile *Daily Register,* May 27, 1893, February 11, 1896; New Orleans *Daily Picayune,* May 25, September 23, 1893, July 31, 1897. Another individual was arrested on bogus testimony at Albany, Georgia, in July 1898; see Atlanta *Constitution,* July 20, 1898.

8. Pensacola *Daily News,* July 20, 1895; New Orleans *Daily Picayune,* May 24, 1893; Mobile *Daily Register,* May 25, 1893, April 12, 1895; New Orleans *Times-Democrat,* April 11, 1895.

9. Carmer, *Stars Fell on Alabama,* 122–25.

Chapter 6. Gunfight at Hurricane Bayou

1. Potter, *Brief History of Escambia County, Alabama,* 10.

2. State of Florida, *Acts and Resolutions, 1893,* 71–72.

3. Atmore *Advance,* December 3, 1931. Brooks stated the attempted arrest was in early summer 1895. But Railroad Bill was infamous by then, thus Brooks was probably thinking early summer 1894.

4. Ibid.; San Saba *News,* June 19, 1891.

5. Atmore *Advance,* December 3, 1931; Montgomery *Daily Advertiser,* March 7, 1895; New Orleans *Times-Democrat,* April 8, 1895.

6. Harlan, "Railroad Bill," 30.

7. Mobile *Daily Register,* August 14, 1894.

8. Ibid.

9. Ibid.

10. Ibid.

11. Ibid.

12. Ibid.; Mobile *Daily Register,* August 28, August 29, 1894; New Orleans *Times-Democrat,* August 14, August 29, 1894.

13. New Orleans *Times-Democrat,* August 29, 1894; Montgomery *Daily Advertiser,* March 7, 1895; Mobile *Daily Register,* August 23, 1894.

14. New Orleans *Times-Democrat*, August 14, August 29, 1894; Montgomery *Daily Advertiser*, April 11, 1895; Greenville *Advocate*, July 10, 1895.

15. Mobile *Daily Register*, October 30, 1894; New Orleans *Daily Picayune*, October 29, 1894. The *Daily Picayune* implies October 28, but the newspaper typically included the previous day's news from Mobile in a special section, usually unadjusted for the time delay.

16. New Orleans *Daily Picayune*, October 29, 1894; Mobile *Daily Register*, October 30, 1894.

17. Mobile *Daily Register*, January 27, 1895; Pensacola *Daily News*, January 30, 1895; New Orleans *Times-Democrat*, October 28, 1894, January 28, 1895; Montgomery *Daily Advertiser*, January 11, 1895.

18. Mobile *Daily Register*, January 27, 1895; New Orleans *Times-Democrat*, January 28, January 29, 1895.

19. Mobile *Daily Register*, January 27, January 29, 1895; Pensacola *Daily News*, January 30, 1895.

20. Mobile *Daily Register*, January 27, January 29, 1895; New Orleans *Times-Democrat*, January 29, 1895; Montgomery *Daily Advertiser*, January 29, 1895; Pensacola *Daily News*, January 30, 1895. Reports of this incident varied significantly, making interpretation difficult; Robert Wilking, noted in the Pensacola *Daily News*, January 30, may have been a typographical error for Robert Wilkins, who would appear later in the story.

21. Pensacola *Daily News*, January 30, 1895; Mobile *Daily Register*, January 29, 1895; New Orleans *Times-Democrat*, January 28, January 29, 1895.

22. Mobile *Daily Register*, January 29, 1895.

23. Ibid.; Montgomery *Daily Advertiser*, January 30, 1895; Pensacola *Daily News*, January 30, 1895.

24. Mobile *Daily Register*, January 29, 1895, March 8, 1896; Montgomery *Daily Advertiser*, March 7, 1895, March 8, 1896.

25. Montgomery *Daily Advertiser*, March 7, 1895; Mobile *Daily Register*, March 8, 1896.

26. Mobile *Daily Register*, March 8, 1896; Montgomery *Daily Advertiser*, March 7, 1895.

27. Montgomery *Daily Advertiser*, March 7, 1895; Mobile *Daily Register*, March 8, 1896.

28. Montgomery *Daily Advertiser*, March 7, 1895; Atlanta *Constitution*, April 8, 1895.

29. Montgomery *Daily Advertiser*, March 7, 1895; Mobile *Daily Register*, March 8, 1896.

30. Montgomery *Daily Advertiser*, March 7, 1895; Mobile *Daily Register*, March 8, 1896.

31. Mobile *Daily Register*, March 8, 1896.

32. Ibid.

33. Montgomery *Daily Advertiser*, March 10, March 12, 1895; *Eastern Shore Courier*, June 2, 1977. The Saturday Railroad Bill was at the Phillips home must have been the same Saturday he was at the Williamson home. At both residences, he was seeking a rifle.

34. Montgomery *Daily Advertiser*, March 12, 1895. Crosby must have been part of the bridge crew, since Cammack did not name him as being one of his crewmen.

Chapter 7. Gunfight at Stewart's Barn

1. Montgomery *Daily Advertiser*, March 12, 1895; Atlanta *Constitution*, March 13, 1895.

2. Mobile *Daily Register*, April 9, 1895.

3. Ibid.; Montgomery *Daily Advertiser*, March 8, 1896; New Orleans *Daily Picayune*, March 8, 1895; Mobile *Daily Register*, April 9, 1895.

4. Montgomery *Daily Advertiser*, March 8, 1896; New Orleans *Daily Picayune*, April 8, 1895; Mobile *Daily Register*, April 9, 1895; New Orleans *Times-Democrat*, April 8, 1895.

5. Montgomery *Daily Advertiser*, March 8, 1896.

6. Ibid.

7. Ibid.; New Orleans *Times-Democrat*, April 8, 1895.

8. Montgomery *Daily Advertiser*, March 8, 1896.

9. Ibid.

10. New Orleans *Times-Democrat*, April 8, 1895.

11. Montgomery *Daily Advertiser*, March 8, 1896.

12. Mobile *Daily Register*, April 9, 1895.

13. Ibid.

14. Atlanta *Constitution*, April 11, 1895.

Chapter 8. The Death of Mark Stinson

1. Harlan, "Railroad Bill," 30.

2. Montgomery *Daily Advertiser*, March 8, 1896. This lengthy article, published immediately after Railroad Bill's death, indicated that L&N's negotiations with Austin and Stinson occurred in September and October 1895, but that would have been after Stinson's death. They probably occurred in September and October 1894.

3. Ibid.

4. Ibid.

5. Ibid.

6. Ibid.

7. Ibid.; Brewton *Pine Belt News*, April 9, 1895.

8. Brewton *Standard Gauge*, December 29, 1898; Harlan, "Railroad Bill," 31.

9. Montgomery *Daily Advertiser*, April 18, 1895.

10. Ibid.

11. Ibid.

12. Ibid.; Mobile *Daily Register*, April 19, 1895.

13. "Geronimo," www.encyclopediaofalabama.org.

14. New Orleans *Daily Picayune*, April 20, 1895; Mobile *Daily Register*, April 18, 1895; Montgomery *Daily Advertiser*, April 17, 1895.

15. New Orleans *Daily Picayune*, April 20, 1895; Montgomery *Daily Advertiser*, April 20, 1895.

16. Montgomery *Daily Advertiser*, April 17, April 18, 1895; Mobile *Daily Register*, April 19, 1895; Atlanta *Constitution*, April 16, 1895.

17. Montgomery *Daily Advertiser*, April 18, 1895; Birmingham *Age-Herald*, April 19, 1895.

18. Montgomery *Daily Advertiser*, April 18, 1895; Mobile *Daily Register*, April 19, 1895.

19. Montgomery *Daily Advertiser*, April 17, 1895; Atlanta *Constitution*, April 16, 1895; Middleton (N.Y.) *Daily Argus*, April 17, 1895.

20. Birmingham *Age-Herald*, April 19, 1895; Montgomery *Daily Advertiser*, April 18, 1895.

21. Mobile *Daily Register*, April 19, 1895; Montgomery *Daily Advertiser*, April 18, 1895.

22. Mobile *Daily Register*, April 19, 1895; Montgomery *Daily Advertiser*, April 18, 1895.

23. Montgomery *Daily Advertiser*, March 8, 1896, December 17, 1905; Brewton *Standard Gauge*, March 12, 1896.

Chapter 9. The Murder of Sheriff Edward McMillan

1. Montgomery *Daily Advertiser*, April 18, April 20, 1895; Mobile *Daily Register*, April 18, 1895; New Orleans *Daily Picayune*, April 18, 1895; Atlanta *Constitution*, April 19, 1895.

2. Montgomery *Daily Advertiser*, April 18, April 20, 1895; Birmingham *Age-Herald*, April 19, 1895; Mobile *Daily Register*, April 19, 1895; New Orleans *Daily Picayune*, April 20, 1895.

3. New Orleans *Daily Picayune*, April 20, 1895; Montgomery *Daily Advertiser*, April 18, April 20, 1895.

4. Pensacola *Daily News*, July 5, 1895.

5. Ibid.; Mobile *Daily Register*, July 9, 1895, March 8, 1896; Scribner, "Short History of Brewton," 10; Brewton *Standard Gauge*, July 4, 1895.

6. *Memorial Record of Alabama*, 986–87; Scribner, "Short History of Brewton," 73.

7. Montgomery *Daily Advertiser*, March 8, 1896; Harlan, "Railroad Bill," 30; Brewton *Standard Gauge*, July 11, 1895.

8. James I. McKinney to Ed McMillan, June 28, 1895, W. McMillan Trust, Brewton, Alabama.

9. Montgomery *Daily Advertiser*, August 6, 1895; Brewton *Pine Belt News*, June 18, July 9, 1895.

10. Montgomery *Daily Advertiser*, July 4, July 5, 1895, March 8, 1896; McKinney to McMillan, June 28, 1895.

11. Pensacola *Daily News*, July 4, 1895; Mobile *Daily Register*, July 5, 1895; Brewton *Standard Gauge*, July 4, 1895.

12. Gordon Beech to Edward Leigh McMillan, June 18, 1976, D. W. McMillan Trust, Brewton, Alabama.

13. Ibid.; Mobile *Daily Register*, July 9, 1895; Pensacola *Daily News*, July 6, 1895.

14. Pensacola *Daily News*, July 6, 1895; Mobile *Daily Register*, July 9, 1895; Baldwin *Times*, July 11, 1895.

15. Birmingham *Age-Herald*, July 4, 1895; Atmore *Advance*, December 3, 1931; Pensacola *Daily News*, July 5, 1895.

16. Atmore *Advance*, December 3, 1931; Pensacola *Daily News*, July 5, July 6, 1895; Brewton *Standard Gauge*, July 4, 1895; Mobile *Daily Register*, July 9, 1895.

17. Mobile *Daily Register*, July 9, 1895; New Orleans *Times-Democrat*, July 9, 1895; Baldwin *Times*, July 11, 1895; Pensacola *Daily News*, July 8, July 9, July 10, July 20, 1895; Beech to McMillan, June 18, 1976.

18. Brewton *Standard Gauge*, July 4, 1895; New Orleans *Times-Democrat*, July 10, 1895; Baldwin *Times*, July 11, 1895; Mobile *Daily Register*, July 9, 1895; Atmore *Advance*, December 3, 1931; Monroe *Journal*, May 17, 1894; Pensacola *Daily News*, July 5, 1895.

19. Pensacola *Daily News*, July 5, July 6, 1895; Mobile *Daily Register*, July 9, 1895, March 8, 1896; Brewton *Standard Gauge*, July 4, 1895.

20. Pensacola *Daily News*, July 4, July 6, 1895; *Florida Times-Union*, July 5, 1895; Mobile *Daily Register*, July 5, 1895.

21. Brewton *Standard Gauge*, July 4, 1895; Montgomery *Daily Advertiser*, July 4, 1895; New Orleans *Times-Democrat*, July 10, 1895; New Orleans *Daily Picayune*, July 5, 1895.

22. Brewton *Pine Belt News*, July 9, 1895.

23. Allison Sinrod, interview by the author, June 12, 2012, at W. D. McMillan Trust, Brewton, Alabama.

Chapter 10. Dragnet in the Panhandle

1. Pensacola *Daily News*, July 4, July 5, 1895; Brewton *Pine Belt News*, July 9, 1895; Mobile *Daily Register*, July 4, July 5, 1895; New Orleans *Times-Democrat*, July 5, 1895; Jacksonville *Times-Union*, July 5, 1895.

2. Greenville *Advocate*, July 10, 1895; *Florida Times-Union*, July 5, 1895; Pensacola *Daily News*, July 5, July 6, 1895; Mobile *Daily Register*, July 5, 1895.

3. *Florida Times-Union*, July 5, 1895; Mobile *Daily Register*, July 5, 1895; New Orleans *Times-Democrat*, July 5, 1895; Pensacola *Daily News*, July 5, 1895.

4. Pensacola *Daily News*, July 5, 1895; New Orleans *Times-Democrat*, July 5, 1895.

5. Pensacola *Daily News*, July 5, July 8, 1895.

6. Pensacola *Daily News*, July 8, 1895.

7. Mobile *Daily Register*, July 9, 1895; Brewton *Standard Gauge*, July 4, 1895; Florida *Times-Union*, July 5 1895.

8. Birmingham *Age-Herald*, July 10, 1895; Mobile *Daily Register*, Tuesday, July 9, 1895; Brewton *Pine Belt News*, July 9, 1895.

9. Greenville *Advocate*, July 10, 1895.

10. Birmingham *Age-Herald*, July 6, 1895.

11. Mobile *Daily Register*, July 11, 1895.

12. Mobile *Daily Register*, August 11, 1895.

13. Montgomery *Daily Advertiser*, July 13, 1895.

14. Birmingham *Age-Herald*, July 6, July 10, 1895; New Orleans *Daily Picayune*, July 16, 1895.

15. Pensacola *Daily News*, July 13, 1895.

16. Atlanta *Constitution*, July 22, 1895; Brewton *Standard Gauge*, July 18, 1985; New Orleans *Daily Picayune*, August 10, 1895; Biloxi *Daily Herald*, August 3, 1895.

17. New Orleans *Daily Picayune*, July 26, 1895; Mobile *Daily Register*, July 27, 1895.

Chapter 11. The Castleberry Chase

1. Mobile *Daily Register*, July 31, 1895; Birmingham *Age-Herald*, August 1, 1895; Covington *Times*, August 2, 1895; Pensacola *Daily News*, August 2, 1895.

2. Pensacola *Daily News*, August 2, 1895; Brewton *Pine Belt News*, August 6, 1895.

3. Mobile *Daily Register*, July 31, 1895; Birmingham *Age-Herald*, August 1, 1895.

4. Pensacola *Daily News*, August 2, 1895.

5. Covington *Times*, August 2, 1895; Mobile *Daily Register*, July 31, 1895;

Pensacola *Daily News*, July 31, August 2, 1895; Birmingham *Age–Herald*, August 1, 1895.

6. Mobile *Daily Register*, July 31, 1895; Brewton *Pine Belt News*, August 6, 1895; Birmingham *Age–Herald*, August 1, 1895; Pensacola *Daily News*, August 2, 1895.

7. Des Moines *Daily Iowa Capital*, October 23, 1897.

8. Pensacola *Daily News*, August 2, 1895; Mobile *Daily Register*, July 31; Birmingham *Age–Herald*, August 1, 1895; Covington *Times*, August 2, 1895; Columbia (S.C.) *State*, August 2, 1895. The Montgomery *Daily Advertiser*, August 2, 1895, indicates two hounds were killed but most articles indicate that Railroad Bill only shot at the pack on July 30.

9. Mobile *Daily Register*, July 31, 1895; Covington *Times*, August 2, 1895.

10. Mobile *Daily Register*, July 31, 1895; Covington *Times*, August 2, 1895; Pensacola *Daily News*, August 2, 1895.

11. Montgomery *Daily Advertiser*, August 1, 1895.

12. Montgomery *Daily Advertiser*, August 1, 1895.

13. Covington *Times*, August 2, 1895; Birmingham *Age–Herald*, August 2, 1895; Atlanta *Constitution*, August 2, 1895; Montgomery *Daily Advertiser*, August 2, 1895; Mobile *Daily Register*, August 2, 1895.

14. New Orleans *Daily Picayune*, August 2, 1895; Mobile *Daily Register*, August 2, 1895; Pensacola *Daily News*, August 3, 1895.

15. New Orleans *Daily Picayune*, June 3, 1896; Mobile *Daily Register*, August 2, 1895; Pensacola *Daily News*, August 3, 1895.

16. Birmingham *Age-Herald*, August 2, 1895; Montgomery *Daily Advertiser*, August 2, 1895.

17. Pensacola *Daily News*, August 3, 1895; Birmingham *Age-Herald*, August 2, 1895; Montgomery *Daily Advertiser*, August 2, 1895.

18. Mobile *Daily Register*, April 9, August 2, 1895; Montgomery *Daily Advertiser*, July 6, 1895; Florida *Times-Union*, August 2, 1895; Brewton *Standard Gauge*, July 18, 1985.

19. Mobile *Daily Register*, August 2, 1895; Birmingham *Age-Herald*, August 2, 1895; Montgomery *Daily Advertiser*, August 2, 1895; Pensacola *Daily News*, August 3, 1895; Brewton *Pine Belt News*, August 6, 1895.

20. Mobile *Daily Register*, August 2, 1895; Brewton *Pine Belt News*, August 6, 1895; Montgomery *Daily Advertiser*, August 2, 1895; Birmingham *Age-Herald*, August 2, 1895.

21. Montgomery *Daily Advertiser*, August 6, 1895.

22. Montgomery *Daily Advertiser*, August 3, 1895; New Orleans *Daily Picayune*, August 2, 1895; Birmingham *Age-Herald*, August 2, 1895; Atlanta *Constitution*, August 2, 1895.

23. Mobile *Daily Register*, August 3, August 4, 1895; Montgomery *Daily Advertiser*, August 3, 1895.

24. Montgomery *Daily Advertiser*, August 6, 1895.

25. Brewton *Pine Belt News*, August 6, 1895.

26. Montgomery *Daily Advertiser*, August 6, 1895.

27. Montgomery *Daily Advertiser*, August 7, 1895.

28. Montgomery *Daily Advertiser*, August 6, 1895.

29. Monroe *Journal*, August 8, 1895.

30. Birmingham *Age-Herald*, August 9, 1895.

31. Mobile *Daily Register*, August 11, 1895.

32. New Orleans *Daily Picayune*, August 10, 1895.

33. Mobile *Daily Register*, August 11, 1895; Montgomery *Daily Advertiser*, August 13, 1895; New Orleans *Daily Picayune*, August 13, 1895; Atlanta *Constitution*, August 13, 1895.

Chapter 12. Unintended Victims

1. Pensacola *Daily News*, July 13, 1895; Brewton *Pine Belt News*, July 13, 1895; New Orleans *Daily Picayune*, July 14, 1895.

2. Mobile *Daily Register*, July 16, 1895; Pensacola *Daily News*, July 13, 1895.

3. Mobile *Daily Register*, July 16, 1895; Pensacola *Daily News*, July 13, 1895.

4. Mobile *Daily Register*, July 16, 1895; Pensacola *Daily News*, July 13, 1895.

5. Mobile *Daily Register*, July 16, 1895; Pensacola *Daily News*, July 13, 1895.

6. Brewton *Pine Belt News*, July 13, 1895; Mobile *Daily Register*, July 16, 1895; New Orleans *Daily Picayune*, July 15, 1895.

7. New Orleans *Daily Picayune*, July 20, 1895.

8. Montgomery *Daily Advertiser*, August 17, 1895; New Orleans *Daily Picayune*, August 17, 1895; Atlanta *Constitution*, August 17, 1895.

9. Montgomery *Daily Advertiser*, August 17, 1895, March 8, 1896.

10. Montgomery *Daily Advertiser*, August 17, 1895.

11. Ibid.; Atlanta *Constitution*, August 20, 1895.

12. Montgomery *Daily Advertiser*, August 17, 1895, March 8, 1896.

13. Montgomery *Daily Advertiser*, August 17, 1895; Atlanta *Constitution*, August 18, 1895; Pensacola *Daily News*, August 19, 1895; Birmingham *Age-Herald,* August 17, 1895.

14. Montgomery *Daily Advertiser*, August 17, 1895; Pensacola *Daily News*, August 19, 1895; Atlanta *Constitution*, August 20, 1895.

15. Birmingham *Age-Herald,* August 17, 1895; Pensacola *Daily News*, August 19, 1895.

16. Mobile *Daily Register*, March 21, 1890, May 25, 1893; New Orleans *Daily Picayune*, July 31, 1897; Montgomery *Daily Advertiser*, April 10, 1895; Pensacola *Daily News*, August 19, 1895.

Chapter 13. The Death of Railroad Bill

1. Mobile *Daily Register*, August 20, 1895; Pensacola *Daily News*, August 19, 1895.

2. Mobile *Daily Register*, August 20, 1895.

3. Ibid.

4. Ibid.

5. Ibid.

6. Ibid.

7. Ibid.

8. Ibid.

9. Birmingham *Age-Herald*, October 20, November 29, 1895; New Orleans *Daily Picayune*, October 28, 1895.

10. Birmingham *Age-Herald*, November 29, 1895; Mobile *Daily Register*, January 3, 1896.

11. Atlanta *Constitution*, January 1, 1896; New Orleans *Daily Picayune*, January 1, 1896.

12. Mobile *Daily Register*, March 8, 1896.

13. Harlan, "Railroad Bill," 69; Montgomery *Daily Advertiser*, March 8, 1896.

14. Mobile Daily Register, March 8, 1896; New Orleans *Times-Democrat*, March 8, 1896; Baldwin *Times*, March 7, 1896.

15. Mobile *Daily Register*, March 8, 1896; Atlanta *Constitution*; February 27, March 8, 1896; New Orleans *Times-Democrat*, March 8, March 9, 1896; Pensacola *Daily News*, March 9, 1896.

16. Pensacola *Daily News*, March 9, 1896; Brewton *Pine Belt News*, March 10, 1896; Brewton *Standard Gauge*, March 12, 1896; New Orleans *Times-Democrat*, March 8, 1896; Atlanta *Constitution*; February 27, 1896. The Atlanta *Constitution* on February 27 reported the existence of Payne's map, about a week before the raid; the Pensacola *Daily News* on March 9 reported that Payne was still in confinement at Brewton.

17. Brewton *Standard Gauge*, March 12, 1896; Brewton *Pine Belt News*, March 10, 1896; Covington *Times*, Friday, March 13, 1896; New Orleans *Daily Picayune*, March 8, 1896; Evergreen *Courant*, March 13, 1896. The general store was located in what is now the one hundred block of Ashley Street.

18. Covington *Times*, March 13, 1896; Brewton *Pine Belt News*, March 10, 1896; Pensacola *Daily News*, March 14, 1896; Harlan, "Railroad Bill," 69. The *Pine Belt News*, March 10, 1896, credits Harlan and Watts with Caldwell's arrest, while the Pensacola *Daily News*, March 14, 1896, credits Allen Brewton. It was probably a joint effort with Brewton having local arrest authority.

19. Pensacola *Daily News*, March 14, 1896; Mobile *Daily Register*, March 8,

1896; Harlan, "Railroad Bill," 69, 70. In criminal court, Caldwell pled guilty and received a sentence of five years in the state penitentiary.

20. Montgomery *Daily Advertiser*, March 8, 1896.

21. Ibid.

22. Brewton *Standard Gauge*, March 12, 1896; New Orleans *Times-Democrat*, March 9, 1896; Brewton *Pine Belt News*, March 10, 1896.

23. A photo of Tidmore and Ward's store is in the Atmore *Spectrum*, December 5, 1907.

24. Brewton *Pine Belt News*, March 10, 1896; Brewton *Standard Gauge*, March 12, 1896; Greenville *Advocate*, March 11, 1896; Evergreen (Ala.) *Courant*, March 13, 1896; Pensacola *Daily News*, March 9, 1896; New Orleans *Daily Picayune*, March 8, 1896; Montgomery *Daily Advertiser*, March 8, 1896; Philadelphia *Inquirer*, March 9, 1896; State of Florida, "An Act to Authorize the Payment of Two Hundred Dollars," 1901, 199.

25. Brewton *Standard Gauge*, March 12, 1896.

26. Ibid.; Montgomery *Daily Advertiser*, July 6, 1895; Evergreen *Courant*, March 13, 1896. A photograph of the desperado after death shows him clean shaven except for a small mustache. The same photograph shows a handmade shoulder strap. The Brewton *Pine Belt News*, March 10, noted one pistol, while the Montgomery *Daily Advertiser*, March 8, 1896, noted two. A second revolver may have been removed before the Brewton reporter arrived.

27. Mobile *Daily Register*, March 8, 1896.

28. Brewton *Standard Gauge*, March 12, 1896; Brewton *Pine Belt News*, March 10, 1896; Baldwin *Times*, March 7, 1896. The .32-caliber rifle McGowin used to kill Railroad Bill is on display at the Thomas E. McMillan Museum, Brewton, Alabama.

29. Brewton *Standard Gauge*, March 12, 1896.

30. New Orleans *Times-Democrat*, March 9, 1896; Evergreen *Courant*, March 13, 1896; Greenville *Advocate*, March 11, 1896; Montgomery *Daily Advertiser*, March 10, 1896; Pensacola *Daily News*, March 9, 1896; Brewton *Standard Gauge*, March 12, 1896.

31. Brewton *Pine Belt News*, March 10, 1896; New Orleans *Times-Democrat*, March 9, 1896.

32. Brewton *Standard Gauge*, March 12, 1896; Harlan, "Railroad Bill," 70; Brewton *Pine Belt News*, March 10, 1896.

33. State of Florida, "An Act to Regulate the Carrying of Firearms," 1893, 71–72; State of Florida, "An Act to Authorize the Payment of Two Hundred Dollars," 1901, 199.

Chapter 14. A Morbid Business

1. Brewton *Pine Belt News*, March 10, 1896.
2. Ibid.; Montgomery *Daily Advertiser*, March 10, 1896.
3. Birmingham *Age Herald*, November 29, 1895; Harlan, "Railroad Bill," 69.
4. Montgomery *Daily Advertiser*, March 10, 1896.
5. Pensacola *Daily News*, March 9, March 12, March 14, 1896.
6. Brewton *Pine Belt News*, March 10, 1896; Pensacola *Daily News*, March 31, 1896; photograph of Railroad Bill in death.
7. New Orleans *Times-Democrat*, March 11, 1896; Brewton *Pine Belt News*, March 10, 1896; Brewton *Standard Gauge*, March 12, 1896.
8. Atlanta *Constitution*, March 10, 1896; Montgomery *Daily Advertiser*, March 10, 1896.
9. Atlanta *Constitution*, March 19, 1896; Mobile *Daily Register*, October 10, 1890; Montgomery *Daily Advertiser*, March 13, 1896. Viewing for profit must have begun the day after arriving, since the body was in the city March 9–13 and exhibited for profit for "four or five days."
10. Montgomery *Daily Advertiser*, March 13, 1896.
11. Pensacola *Daily News*, March 12, March 14, 1896; Jacksonville *Times-Union*, March 14, 1896.
12. Pensacola *Daily News*, March 14, 1896; *Florida Times-Union*, March 14, 1896; Brewton *Pine Belt News*, March 10, 1896.
13. Pensacola *Daily News*, March 14, 1896 (two articles); Atlanta *Constitution*, March 19, 1896.
14. Mobile *Daily Register*, March 17, 1896; Atlanta *Constitution*, March 19, 1896; New Orleans *Daily Picayune*, March 17, 1896.
15. Pensacola *Daily News*, March 30, March 31, 1896; Brewton *Standard Gauge*, April 2, 1896; Atlanta *Constitution*, April 1, 1896.
16. Atlanta *Constitution*, April 1, 1896.

Conclusion: Endless Folklore

1. Carmer, *Stars Fell on Alabama*, 122.
2. Montgomery *Daily Advertiser*, August 7, 1895.
3. Ibid.
4. Ibid.
5. Ibid.
6. Ibid.
7. Edward Leigh McMillan to R. W. Gordon, October 12, 1927, Gordon MS 3442, Robert W. Gordon Manuscript Collection, Library of Congress, American Folklife Center, Washington, D.C.

8. Ibid.; Montgomery *Daily Advertiser*, April 10, 1895.

9. *Atlantic Monthly*, January 1895, 136; Mobile *Daily Register*, March 9, 1895.

10. Montgomery *Daily Advertiser*, December 17, 1905; Harlan, "Railroad Bill," 30–31, 69–70; Penick, "Railroad Bill," 86; Carmer, *Stars Fell on Alabama*, 122–25; Figh, "Nineteenth Century Outlaws in Alabama Folklore," 126–35; Scribner, "Short History of Brewton," 73–79; McLendon, "Accounts of Escambia County's Railroad Bill," 6–12; Roberts, "'Railroad Bill' and the American Outlaw Tradition," 315–28; Mathews, "'Looking for Railroad Bill,'" 66–68; Cohen, *Long Steel Rail*, 122.

11. Odum, "Folk-Song and Folk-Poetry," 256, 289.

12. Ibid., 289–90.

13. "Railroad Bill," Gordon MS 3790, Anonymous 11, Robert Winslow Gordon Manuscript Collection, American Folklife Center, Library of Congress, Washington, D.C.

14. Cohen, *Long Steel Rail*, 127; "Railroad Bill," www.fresnostate.edu/folklore/ballads/LI13.html.

15. London *Telegraph*, August 18, 2014; Sara Greek, "Lonnie Donegan Jnr to Perform at Hertford Theatre," August 20, 2014, www.hertfordshiremercury.co.uk/Lonnie-Donegan-Jnr-perform-Hertford-Theatre/story-22787989-detail/story.html.

Bibliography

Agee, George. *Rube Burrow, King of Outlaws, and His Band of Train Robbers: An Accurate and Faithful History of Their Exploits and Adventures.* Chicago: Henneberry Co., 1890.

"Alabama's Tramp Law." *Railway Conductor* 18 (1901): 27–28.

Carmer, Carl. *Stars Fell on Alabama.* New York: Blue Ribbon Books, 1934.

Cohen, Norm. *Long Steel Rail: The Railroad in American Folksong.* Urbana: University of Illinois Press, 2000.

"The Collector's Club: Some Negro Superstitions." *Atlantic Monthly*, January 1895, 136–40.

Figh, Margaret Gillis. "Nineteenth Century Outlaws in Alabama Folklore." *Southern Folklore Quarterly* 1 (March 1937): 126–35.

Flynt, Josiah. "The Tramp and the Railroads." *Century Magazine*, June 1899, 258–66.

Harlan, John B. "Railroad Bill." *The L. & N. Employes' [sic] Magazine*, May 1927, 30–31, 69–70.

Mathews, Burgin. "'Looking for Railroad Bill': On the Trail of an Alabama Badman." *Southern Cultures* 9, no. 3 (Fall 2003): 66–88.

McLendon, Carolyn Pugh. "Accounts of Escambia County's Railroad Bill." *Escambia County Historical Quarterly* 5, no. 4 (December 1977): 6–12.

Memorial Record of Alabama. Vol. 1. 1893. Spartanburg, S.C.: The Reprint Company, 1976.

Mobile City Directory. Annual reprints, 1882–1885. Local History and Genealogy Division, Mobile Public Library, Mobile, Alabama.

Odum, Howard W. "Folk-Song and Folk-Poetry as Found in the Secular Songs of the Southern Negroes." *Journal of American Folk-Lore* 24 (July–September 1911): 255–94.

Penick, James. "Railroad Bill." *Gulf Coast Historical Review* 10, no. 1 (Fall 1994): 85–92.

Potter, Henderson A. *A Brief History of Escambia County, Alabama.* N.p., n.d.

Rezneck, Samuel. "Unemployment, Unrest, and Relief in the United States during the Depression of 1893–97." *Journal of Political Economy* 61, no. 4 (1953): 324–45.

Roberts, John W. "'Railroad Bill' and the American Outlaw Tradition." *Western Folklore* 40, no. 4 (October 1981): 315–28.

Scribner, R. L. "A Short History of Brewton, Alabama." *Alabama Historical Quarterly* 11, nos. 1–4 (1949): 73–79.

State of Alabama. *Acts of the General Assembly of Alabama, Passed at the Session of 1894–5.* Montgomery, 1895.

State of Florida. "An Act to Authorize the Payment of Two Hundred Dollars, the Reward Offered by the Governor of Florida, for the Capture of Outlaw Morris Slater." *Regular Session, 1901: Acts and Resolutions Adopted by the Legislature of Florida at Its Regular Session (April 2 to May 31, 1901) under the Constitution of A.D. 1885.* Tallahassee, 1901.

———. "An Act to Regulate the Carrying of Firearms." *Regular Session, 1893: Acts and Resolutions Adopted by the Legislature of Florida at Its Fourth Regular Session under the Constitution of A.D. 1885.* Tallahassee, 1893.

Svenvold, Mark. *Elmer McCurdy: The Misadventures in Life and Afterlife of an American Outlaw.* New York: Basic Books, 2002.

Larry L. Massey is an independent writer and researcher living in Mobile, Alabama, and DeLand, Florida. His interest in family and regional history led to a six-year study of Railroad Bill. The outlaw and former turpentine worker once worked with Massey's great-great-grandfather at Bluff Springs, Florida.